WAKE OF THE GREAT SEALERS

Text by Farley Mowat **WAKE OF THE GREAT SEALERS**

Prints and drawings by David Blackwood

McCLELLAND AND STEWART LIMITED

The Canadian Publishers
McClelland and Stewart Limited
Illustrated Book Division
25 Hollinger Road, Toronto

PRINTED AND BOUND IN CANADA

AUTHOR'S NOTE Apart from the material in this book which is credited to an actual source, the text is my own, derived from my own researches and from many conversations with Newfoundland sealers. For literary purposes, I have presented much of it in the first person and have given fictional attributions to the narrators. However, the material itself is in no way invented, but is the remembered and the recorded truth about the great seal hunt of Newfoundland.

I was born out of them – and into them – part of the seventh generation to make a new beginning within an old continuity in that great bight of Newfoundland's northeast coast called Bonavista Bay.

Ours was a timeless way of life. Three centuries ago when our ancestors crossed the Western Ocean they had already been committed to the sea since time out of memory. They neither knew, nor wished for, any way of life not of the sea. Because the land meant little to them, except as a place to rest, procreate, build one's vessel, or repair one's gear, they did not greatly care what kind of land it was. As long as it was washed by fruitful waters, any bald lump of an islet or rocky cleft on the mainland shore was good enough.

My people were sea-hunters and the two great quarries of these cold northern seas were the cod and the seal, so they became cod fishers and sealers, and proud of the calling. My grandfather, who belonged to Swains Tickle, was a man who knew the stuff of which our pride was made.

From earliest times in the sealing game, or fishing down the Labrador, we fellows was always to the fore. Good seamen we had to be. Schooner men as could take a vessel any place and bring her back, for we was cut off from the world all ways around, but on the water – which was froze harder than the hobs of hell the big part of the year. The ocean was our highroad; aye, there was no other, whether we was bound up for St. John's town laden with salt cod or seal pelts or away to visit one of our own places: Badgers Quay, Pinchards Bight, Braggs Island, Mortons Harbour, or Greenspond maybe. Them was all independent places. And independent people we was too, no matter was you a foreign-going captain, master of a sealing ship, a Labrador schooner skipper, or an inshore fisherman with not much more to show for yourself than a leaky skiff and half a share in an old cod trap....

...Aunt Gerti Hann was a proper yary woman, the daughter of Captain Billy Winsor, a jowler of a sealing skipper as ever was. He made a big lot of money and built a house fit for a prince. 'Twas him turned over the name Swains Tickle. Said it warn't fittin' for a place as smart as our'n. So, being a good Methodist, he called it Wesleyville and the name held –for all but Aunt Gerti. "The Captain can call it Wesleyville, and so can the Good Lord Himself," she used to tell us youngsters, "but I was barn in Swains Tickle, and that's the place I'll lay me down."

Captain Elijah Mullet, now he was a different kettle of fish. He went sealing a good many springs, but his heart was always in the cod fishery down the Labrador. Worked like a dog all of his life, but had no luck at all, and when he passed on after sixty year at the fishery game, he was a poor man. 'Twas like the old song says:

The best you can do is to work with a will,
For when 'tis all finished you're hauled on the hill.
You're hauled on the hill and put down in the cold,
And when 'tis all finished...you're still in the hold!
For 'tis hard, hard times.

When I was a young lad there was an old fellow lived to himself on the point at Claddy-on-Neck. He was barn crippled and never could go to sea nor to the sealing, so he never could call himself a proper man. Some says he turned foolish over it. Times you might spy him on the headland watching out over the sea or the ice. He never said what he was spying after. I doubt anybody ever asked. One April day he was gone out of it. P'raps he went over the cliff. But they's some as thinks the poor fellow tried to go sealing by his own self onto the last of it–walked out on the loose ice when it was going abroad and drowned in the slob.

Winter times we youngsters used to chase one another on the running ice offshore. You had to be quick, jumping from pan to pan, so the ice wouldn't founder under you. 'Twas called copying and 'twas rare sport, and it come in handy when you was old enough to try for a berth on a sealing ship bound off for the northern ice.

Jacob Kelloway, now, he was a proper "swiler," well known all around Bonavist' Bay as a gert hand with a gaff or a tow. He went master watch most of his thirty-seven springs sealing to the northern ice and come through with nary a hurt. Jacob never got clear of the time the doctor on the S.S. Terra Nova sketched him off with a camera. He kept that picture by him till he died, and give orders 'twas to be buried with him, so the angels would know what he looked like in his prime.

The off-lying islands in the northern bays were favoured by our people because they lay handy to the fishing grounds, and that was where our lives were centred. When men had to row, or depend on a little lug sail to get them to and from the fishing, it counted more to be near the grounds than to live in a fine, snug place on shore. The offer islands were stern, unfriendly lumps of rock naked to the pounding seas from the North Atlantic, half-drowned in sprindrift when the nor'easters blew, and cut off from the mainland for weeks and months when the arctic pack drove down amongst them. Yet, wherever they offered any kind of shelter for the boats, there our settlements took root and grew, clinging like limpets between wind and water.

I remember how the little settlement on Braggs Island, where I spent much of my childhood, would come alive before daybreak on a summer's morn. We woke to no belated cock-crow, but to the bark of the single-cylinder "make-and-breaks," as the inshore fishermen called their old engines. The slow, heavy pulse of the explosions was the heartbeat of the place. Skiffs and punts would dawdle awhile in the narrow runs while the men hauled herring nets for their supply of bait. Life wakened all along the landwash, where the surging waters meet the shore. This was the men's domain: docks and stages, spidery flakes for drying fish, storerooms, upended boats, and a clutter of old killock anchors. It was in the storerooms that the gear was kept, nets mended, lines baited – and where, warmed by the glow of little bogey stoves, men who were too old for the fishery gathered early in the day to smoke and gab until the boats came homeward from the sea.

The houses crowded as close to the landwash as they could get and just as close to one another. Linked by meandering paths that never knew a wheel, they and their close-fenced little gardens, manured with seaweed and capelin fish, were the women's world. Children ran amongst the box-square homes that leaned into the tireless winds. Women emerged from their frame fortresses and scuttled the few yards to the merchant's tiny store to buy a pound of salt pork or a packet of tea. A brisk young fellow might stride by, his great-grandfather's muzzle-loader on his shoulder, off for a day's gunning after seabirds. And all day long someone would be going to or coming from the communal well.

When darkness fell, leaving each house isolated and alone, but glowing outwardly through its frilled curtains, the slow and easy flow of human movement would not cease. The lithe shadows of young people would go slipping past, from darkness into darkness, melting and clinging as the night grew old.

Oil lamps burned in every kitchen, and the woodsmoke would stagger from the chimney tops when the fog shroud rolled in, obscuring all the world and waking some distant vessel's horn so that the heavy, questioning voice would boom above the never-ending mutter of the sea:

"We are here . . . AAAAAAAAAH . . . where are you?"

My father and his brothers mostly left the inshore fishery alone.
"Small boats," they used to say," is for small men." For them
the fishery meant sealing in the early spring, and then
the summer voyage to Labrador for cod. June saw
the schooner fleet sail out from every little cove along
the northern coast. From Trinity, all round the shores of Bonavista Bay;
from Fogo, Twillingate, from Notre Dame, and west to Cape St. John,
two or three hundred vessels flying free! All punching to be first
upon the cod-fish grounds down north from Belle Isle Strait
nearly a thousand miles to Chidley Cape. Hundreds of white-winged ships
all racing for the prime trap berths at Domino, Groswater Bay,
Wild Bight, Cut Throat, Cape Harrigan and Makkovik, Nain, Manvers,
Mugford and Saglek, Ramah and Iron Strand. . . . And, when the cod
struck in, then the long northern days – short nights –
hauling the traps; cutting and splitting fish on deck; salting it down,
until the vessel had her "saving crop" and, with good luck,
a bumper voyage. Then, in September month, the ships drove south
like birds, dispersing to the myriad coves from whence they came.

That was one-half of it. The other was the late autumnal voyage
taking the "made fish" (salt bulk or dried) past Baccalieu
and south around to St. John's town. The fish would there be sold;
the merchants' debts repaid, and with what small amount remained
men bought the winter's grub: cases of tea, barrels of flour,
'lasses and butter, and salt pork. When all was stowed below,
the schooners cleared for home. November it would be by then,
with winter storms already battering a snow-smeared coast.
Those were hard times to be at sea, and every year,
the Widow Maker took her toll of men and ships. One June when I was young,
my Uncle Thomas shipped as second hand to Skipper 'Lias Glover,
bound down the Labrador with fifteen sharemen in the schooner *Kindly Light*.

They never was such plenty of fine fish before! We loaded her
right to the hatches, penned a hundred quintal more on deck,
and then bore up for home – the twentieth day of August month it were.
The weather from nor'west and so we made the passage home to Braggs
in just five roaring days. Having no long delay in Bonavista Bay
we cleared again for St. John's town and ran her down in one long reach.
The price of fish was something wonderful that year. When we had
settled up, we took our sharemen's bills and near bought out the place.
Plenty of grub, me sons! Yard goods and ribbands for the women and the maids.
Twine enough for to knit a hundred nets. It looked to be
the bestest voyage we lads had ever seen. We bore away for Braggs
before a sou'east breeze. Next day we raised the white snow-duster
on the Nor'ard Head and altered for the cove...but as we come about
on the new tack the ship heeled over to a sudden heavy gust;
lay down until her rail was under and the scuppers running green.
Up in the fo'c'sle head the galley stove – red hot it were,
for 'twas a bitter day – tore loose; plunged thwartship into a drum of kerosene.
Then come a dreadful sight! Enough to make a dead man stand and stare.
The flames run up to heaven in the time it took for we to man the boats.
We just got clear, and nothing but the clothes we stood up in.
Like a great torch, she went, and not a single thing that mortal man
could do. Up on the Nor'ard Head the people gathered, and they stood
and watched her burn. By the Lard Jasus, byes, it were a cruel cut.
Our whole year's voyage condemned. Hard times for Braggs that day,
when we folk watched the Kindly Light burn down and sink away.

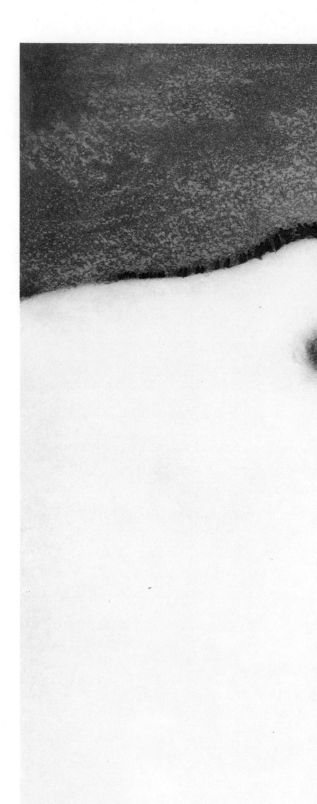

In November of the year when I turned ten my father
put to sea from Wesleyville as master of the topsail schooner
Elsie Blake, bound foreign with a lading of salt fish for Genoa.
We spent that winter with my mother's kin, Ephram and
Gramma Glover, out on Braggs. Only a dozen families clung to that bald rock
but they'd been rooted there a hundred years or more
and were knit up together tight as a school of capelin in a net.
What pleasured any one of them gave pleasure to them all,
and pain for one, was pain for everyone. I well remember how,
early in January – the bay already running thick with drifting ice –
my young first cousin, Millie Feltham, "felt her heart."
And all hands knew that she would likely die unless we could get help.
'Twas easier said than done. The wind was blowing half-a-gale sou'west,
heaving the ice like moving mountains on a freezing sea.
But all the same, five men agreed to try and take a big trap skiff
twelve miles across that grinding waste of ice to Wesleyville.
There was a travelling doctor somewhere on the mainland coast.
They were away three days, and no one did a tap while they were gone,
could think of nothing but the men out there among the floes.
Grandfather Glover – he was one of them. It was his boat.
As hour followed hour, day followed day. Gram Glover waited silent
by the landward window glass, still as a monument,
her mind bound out across that heaving wilderness of ice
'til, out of pity, Mother tried to shift Gram's mind to something else.
"Don't fret yourself so much, me dear. They'm be all right."
Gram Glover turned and took my mother's eye, and softly said:
"A woman's thought has *got* to fly beside her man upon the sea.
Her thought, aye, and her prayers as well. Remember, maid,
It is the least as we can do for them as cares for we."

Cousin Millie Feltham was fifteen when the Braggs Island men brought the doctor and saved her life. And the very next year Josh Barbour "took her walking," as the saying was. He had come out to Braggs from Greenspond for a Christmas visit, being related to the Glovers on his father's side. It was my grandfather, Skipper Ephram, who told us how it all came about.

He were a wandering lad, were Josh, but when he struck onto Millie, why he just took root. We couldn't get clear of he at all. He was still under our roof in March when sealing time come round. Evenings he'd sit by the kitchen stove polishing up his big black boots with our best butter and molasses, and then away he'd go, a-courting.

He would sit in Feltham's kitchen helping Skipper 'Lias knit up twine for salmon nets, but his eye was mostly on the maid, and he spiled a powerful good lot of twine. Going on past midnight, the family would give it up and go off to sleep, leaving Millie and Josh on the two ends of the daybed; and all hands knowed where that was bound to end. Come the time Josh left for a sealing berth aboard the Ranger, 'twas all fixed up for they to be married in November month. After Josh come back from the Labrador fishery in the fall of the year, he shipped for St. John's in a Fogo schooner to buy what gear he needed to set up on his own with Millie. But, homeward bound, that schooner run into a living gale. Took the sticks right out of her and drove her off to sea. 'Twas near two weeks afore the wreck was sighted by a steamer and the crew took off. Trouble was, that steamer was bound for the Argentine and, between the jigs and the reels, Josh never did get home 'til January come around again.

'Course, Millie had got her baby by then – a right strong boy, born with a hood over his head. The finest kind of luck, that was, for a baby born with a hood can never drown. Josh come home too late for the christening of his boy, but in plenty time for a proper wedding!

'Twas a good year for all hands. Lots of fish and a high price, so they was more'n a drop or two on the go. You'd never sniff it in ary house, for the women wouldn't have it; but all we fellows had a bottle hid away. Skipper 'Lias had laid in a keg of black rum against the wedding, and Josh carried home a couple of gallons of that white stuff from St. Pierre...like dynamite it were!

The wedding was called for the first Sunday the minister might happen to visit the island. He'd come two or three times a year for marryings and baptizings. But some folks was not contented to wait for he, and so the corks come out well afore sailing day! One evening down in me own fish store Uncle Abe Oram and Skipper 'Lias set out to find which one of they could jig the longest and the bestest. 'Twas never settled 'cause Uncle Abraham bursted clean through the floor of the room and lost his rubber boots into the landwash.

'Twas dirty weather on the wedding day, with a good breeze blowing off the water and the snow drifting like smoke. Millie wore her Da's big coat over her wedding rig, with her veil a-drawing like a t'gallant sail in the wind. The banging of them old swiling guns was something for to hear, and the smell of the black powder sticks in me nostrils yet. Aye, 'twas the finest kind of wedding Millie and Josh Barbour had that day. Skipper Elias and Aunt Maggie Feltham was some proud of they!

Skipper 'Lias was a high-lining fisherman and swiler all his life
—there was none better as we knew. 'Lias were good for it.
His woman, Maggie, come from the same mould as he.

They was no lighthouse out on Braggs, those times.
Come thick o'fog or starm o'wind and snow,
'twere hard enough to make the land. Many's the vessel and her crew
was lost because of that. Aunt Maggie's poor old dad,
skipper and owner of the coasting schooner John and Jericho,
was inward bound for Braggs one winter ev'ning from St. John's
and missed the offer isle what marks the run. 'Twas thick o'snow
and no man seen the land until it were too late. The vessel drove
onto the sunkers off the Popplestone. And not one soul was saved.

Maggie was only half-ways growed, those times, but old enough
to know her mind. Next day she rousted out we island men
and made us set a spar and tackle on the top of Nor'ard Head.
From that day on, summers and winters, every ev'ning time
she'd fill a lamp—kerosene-fired, with a red glass globe—
her gert cloak swirling in the wind, she'd take her way
in sickness or in health, come starm or sleet, and hist that light
to help poor sailor-men steer homeward through the night.

Skipper Elias and Aunt Mag was married forty-seven year,
and raised a wonderful fine crowd of lads and maids –
five daughters and six sons – and never a one as knew a time of want.
For 'Lias was a driving man, as would have worked
the devil to his grave. Thirty spring seasons to the ice,
and forty summers fishing down the coast of Labrador.
He stayed right up 'til, in his seventy-seventh year,
he took the cancer in his throat. They carried him away
to finish out his voyage in hospital in St. John's town.
Then, for the first time in her life, Aunt Maggie quit our rock
to go along of he, leaving her youngest son to tend the Nor'ard light.

The skipper wasted for a month. His flesh went clean away
to nothing on the last of it, and then Aunt Maggie brought him home.
She travelled with the coffin up to Gambo on the morning train.
Six of we met her there; carried the box aboard John Oram's boat,
and thought to leave for Braggs at once, 'til Aunt Mag spoke:
"I'd take it kindly, could you bide 'til dark," she said,
"So he can see the light shine out once more on Nor'ard Head."

I supposes 'twas a hard life, accordin' to what they says nowadays, but it never seemed so to we. We was all into it, men and maids together. It took strong hearts and hands, but it give us strength in the doing. And 'twas not all work and no play. By November month the year's voyage was wound up–gear stowed away, fish made and shipped, schooners all laid up and gone to sleep. Was nothing for it then but to snug down for the winter. Then come the dances and socials and weddings and concerts in every place, and visiting back and forth all round the bay. Bonfire Night–some calls it Guy Fawkes Day–was always a gert time in Wesleyville, with folk from all around coming along to act out something for the big concert. Aunt Rene Sturge was the rale one! Belonged to Pinchards Bight, she did. She'd clumb onto the stage and do her skit, and 'twould make a dogfish laugh hisself to death. She'd stand up there with a scrubboard and a bucket full of suds, and Uncle Peter Sturge's dirty underclothes, and wash away at they, all the time carrying on about the poor old fellow, making him out to be a proper bosthoon, getting it out on he for the troubles he'd give her all year round....

...But the bestest time of all was Christmas. The fun began New Christmas Day, December 25th, and run right on to Old Christmas Day, January 6th. That was the jollification! For twelve nights there'd be a time to someone's place, a different one each night. And all the while the mummers was on the go. They was dressed up in every sort of guise, with their faces hid so's none would know them. Crowds of mummers would go along from house to house, knocking on the doors and bawling in them squeaky mummers' voices: "Is the mummers 'lowed in?" Once inside they'd pull out a fiddle or maybe a 'cordian and sing a song and start a dance. They'd snatch up the women in the house and dance them 'til their legs give out. People would try to guess who they was, and if they guessed a-right, the mummers was bound to throw back their hoods and show up. Then they'd all drink a drop of stuff with hot water and sugar, and tramp off into the dark again. Ah, yiss, me sons...them was the enjoying times!

During the summer and autumn ours was a world of water, but for most of the rest of the year it was a world of ice. In late November a great tongue of the polar pack began thrusting southward out of Baffin Bay and by Christmas time had pushed right down the coast of Labrador to Belle Isle Strait. By late January it had engulfed all of northern Newfoundland and was even swelling out over the Grand Banks. Then the whole of the seas we sailed in summer were hidden beneath ice fields. Nor'east gales drove the pack tight to our unyielding coasts until the floes began to ride over one another, forming mountainous ridges and compacting the fields until they became one vast, unbroken plain stretching to the farthest horizon. Then westerly gales might drive the ice offshore again until the great white plain cracked and split, allowing leads and lakes of open water, smoking and steaming in the bitter cold, to form between the floes. At night new ice skimmed over the leads; was crushed by the wheeling motion of the pack and formed its own fields of shattered "slob". Here and there, towering bergs plowed through the thickest pack as if it was no more than brittle candy. When the long Atlantic swell set in, the icy plain heaved to the motion until mounded hills and deep, rounded valleys began to crawl slowly across the fields, setting up a terrible conflict that growled like steady thunder, and the cold air glittered with shattered ice crystals.

To those who do not know it, the northern ice fields must appear to be a place that life abhors. But it is really a living world. Long, long ago two kinds of seals, the harps and the hoods, discovered that the ice world offered everything they needed. The rich waters underlying it gave rise to millions of small fishes upon which the seals could feed. The ice gave them a place to rest and to bear and nurture their young, secure from any dangers which might threaten from the land. The harps, who once must have numbered many millions, lived in great companies, hundreds of thousands of them sporting together in the open leads and lakes between the floes, or bearing their young together in vast nurseries that stretched for miles across the wheeling pans. The hoods, larger and not so numerous, preferred to live in family groups consisting of an old dog hood, his bitch, and their single blue-white pup.

The pups of both kinds were born in early March on the southern stretches of their floating world. Three weeks later the young, grown roly-poly on the rich milk of their mothers, were weaned and took to the sea to begin their own independent lives. This was the time when the ice-edge had reached its southern limits and was beginning to shrink northward again under the warmth of the spring sun. The seals drifted north with it, some of them travelling right to the edge of the Arctic Ocean. But when the ice surged south again in autumn, the harp and hood nations rode and swam in its vanguard, repeating an age-old migration which every year took them many thousands of miles.

It was the annual visit of these mighty herds that, as much as anything, led my forebears to make their homes on the bleak coasts of Newfoundland's northern bays. My grandfather used to tell us how it came about.

'Tis often said, and a good many believes in it, as codfish was the whole backbone of Newfoundland. Maybe 'twas so for some parts, and maybe 'tis mainly so these times, but 'twarn't always so.

On the first of it, the people as come to the northern bays was only summer liveyers who come up in their boats in the spring of the year from eastward – from Trinity and Conception Bays for the most part – and were gone out of it again in the fall of the year. They was only after cod; but back two hundred years ago some of them fell onto the seal fishery, and once they had it they never let it go. They took to staying in them little places in the north right through the winter so as to be handy to the seals, and in the end 'twas the seal fishery as built up all them places right round from Cape Bonavista clear to Cape St. John.

It was the French who first took up the seal fishery, although of course the Eskimos and Indians of Newfoundland and Labrador had been catching seals with nets and harpoons for thousands of years before Europeans first came this way. The English were slow to follow the French. Cod was their prime quarry and they were single-minded about it. It was not until some of them, encroaching northwestward into French fishing grounds during summer voyages, found that seals could be an even better source of livelihood, that settlement of the northern bays began. That discovery, and the consequent need to overwinter in order to be on hand when the seals arrived, resulted in the eventual English settlement of the northeastern coast by nearly four hundred little clusters of our people. In spring, summer, and early autumn they mostly fished cod and salmon; but in early January seals became the centre of their lives.

The first settlers in the northern bays took up the net fishery. January was the time when tremendous herds of old dog seals and pregnant bitches came streaming south along the coasts and into the bays, in advance of the ice that was their abiding home. They came in unbelievable numbers. About 1760 a French seal-fisher, wintering on the northern tip of Newfoundland, wrote of seeing a "string" of old seals that filled the sea from the landwash seaward to the limit of his vision, and took ten days and nights to pass.

As soon as the first outriders of the herds were sighted, all the able-bodied men of the northern bays turned out in small boats to set long, heavy seal nets – some of them five hundred feet in length – reaching seaward from the headlands, or strung out between the offshore islands. The commander of a British naval squadron who visited our coast late in the eighteenth century reported the inhabitants then owned at least two thousand of these nets and that seal oil and sealskins accounted for at least half their harvest from the seas.

Not much time passed before our forebears went the French one better and began adding to that winter harvest by gunning for seals in the open leads near shore. In the beginning they went out in open rowboats, but soon they began using larger craft and venturing farther and farther into the ice. By about 1780 they were using shallops, sail boats about thirty feet long with a shelter deck fore and aft, but open amidships. In these little vessels a crew of a half dozen men would sometimes cruise the leads in the bay ice for a week at a time, hunting the old seals with muzzle-loading guns.

Although the hunt with nets and guns was aimed at adult seals, occasionally our people reaped a windfall of a different kind. Once or twice in every generation the pans of whelping ice, laden with new-born "white-coats," would be driven by nor'east gales into contact with the land. Then men, women, children, even dogs, rushed pell-mell out over the raftered ice to reach the nurseries where they made fantastic slaughter of the young seals. They still tell of one such foray over the shorebound ice of Bonavista Bay that yielded 140,000 whitecoat sculps – a sculp being the pelt with the underlying layers of fat still attached.

Happenstances such as this whetted the appetite of the more daring men, and they began trying to reach the whelping ice in their shallops. Sometimes they were lucky. More times both men and boats were crushed and lost. The answer was bigger, stronger vessels and, about 1795, such ships were being built – and so the ship fishery to the ice was born.

In the beginning the ships were small schooners, heavily timbered and strengthened. They were rough, tough little vessels, locally built, and their crews, who were also their builders, were just as rough and tough. A dozen men would set out into the ice in one of these little ships for what might turn out to be a month-long voyage, most of it to be spent drifting helplessly with the pack, their vessel "jammed" and likely to be crushed at any moment. They rarely even had a stove aboard but lived cold and wet, eating uncooked food and drinking melt water from pools on the ice.

The losses suffered by these early men and vessels were terrible. Sometimes a quarter of the ships were lost in a single season. However, those that did reach the nurseries and managed to return brought home such rich cargoes that it was not long before the whole of Newfoundland began to go seal-crazy. Thousands of vessels were built all along the northern and eastern coasts to "prosecute the sealing game." These gradually increased in size until brigs of 150 tons were being built for the ice-hunt. The top of it all came in 1884 when 360 sailing vessels carrying nearly 11,000 sealers (which was the biggest portion of the able-bodied men of the Island), went to the northern ice and brought back 700,000 seal sculps – most of them whitecoats.

The swiling frenzy seemed to mount with each succeeding year – bringing with it appalling losses of ships and men. Between 1810 and 1870 more than 400 sealing vessels were sunk at the ice and, although nobody bothered to keep account of how many men were lost, there must have been well over a thousand drowned, crushed, or frozen to death. They did not die alone. Between 1838 and 1870, the sealing fleet brought in more than twelve million sculps!

The odourless, tasteless oil refined from seal fat commanded premium prices in Europe where it was used for oil lighting, cooking fat, and lubrication. Called "train oil" it was as valuable as whale oil, but the sculps had an additional value since the de-fatted skins made excellent leather. When electricity replaced oil lamps, seal oil continued to increase in value, being used in many industrial processes including the making of high explosives, or as food in the form of margarine.

Swiling eventually came to involve almost every settlement in Newfoundland and, until about the middle of the nineteenth century, it remained a local business with all the people of each settlement taking some part in the ship-building, the hunt, or the preparation of the fat and the skins; and all hands sharing in the returns. Then things began to change. As the profits mounted and the cost of building and outfitting big ships also increased, one or two families in each settlement began to engross the business to themselves. In short enough order they came to own the seal fishery, and the old, communal way of life was lost forever. The sons and grandsons of the men who brought the Newfoundland seal fishery into being – who built it with their hands and their hearts . . . and their lives – sank back to the level of hired men, and underpaid and maltreated ones, at that. A description, written by one of the new outport aristocracy built on seals, gives a little of the flavour of how things were in the swiling game during the last half of the nineteenth century.

«St. Stephen's Day, December 26th, was the day the crews all gathered at the homes of the captains and owners to sign on for the spring hunt. Early in February the crews would begin hauling firewood and logs from the forests, ready to be turned into fuel and into spars and punts for the vessels that would soon be ready to leave for the ice. Their labour was not paid for, but was considered part of the sealers' duty. All the men got out of it was their grub...About February 25th, the captains began to get things ready. March 1st was sailing day. At the first crack of dawn windlasses were manned and sails were hung on the yards ready to sheet-home as soon as the anchor was hove short, each captain eager to be in the lead...It often happened that the harbour was frozen over with from two to four feet of solid ice. All the crews joined together and began sawing a channel to open water. This meant a good deal of labour and occupied ten days or more. As the blocks of ice were sawn they were sunk under the edge of the floes and the ships moved down the channel. With sometimes forty or fifty ships and sixteen hundred men in the parade, it made a great sight. Sometimes when the mouth of the harbour was reached the whole outer bay would still be frozen over. Then there was nothing to do but wait for a swell to heave in and break up the ice. Some years a month went by before the swell would heave in. Mutiny was often at hand in those times due to skippers trying to save on food. Captains were martinets. There was old Bill Whelan, master and owner for many years of the brig Hound. Some declared he had sold himself to the devil. He always began his day with a toddy of rum. Every half-watch he'd have another or so. Blow high, blow low, rain, snow, or frost, from dawn to dark he always kept the deck. When he went below at night he had his skin full, but the next day he was back again, fresh as a rose. His officers were hard as nails, and the Old Man was iron, but with the constant driving of ship and men, he always got the seals.»

-Adapted from The Log of "Bob" Bartlett
by Captain Robert A. Bartlett

The passing of the old, egalitarian way of life in the northern bay settlements and the growth of local aristocracies based largely on wealth from the seals did not go unremarked. In the 1860's a St. John's clergyman, who must have been born well ahead of his age, wrote what was, for those times, a bitter denunciation of the new system.

Even when death at its most fearful puts not a sudden period to the sufferings of the sealer, the toils and hardships and perils of the voyage are indescribable; while he has nought to sustain him but the fond hope of being able to realize a temporary provision for an affectionate wife and children. The seal fishery is a lottery where all is risk and uncertainty, but the risk, we must confess, is not equally distributed. Take for instance a vessel of 120 tons. Her merchant-owner may gain a thousand pounds or more if the voyage prospers. But also involved in her success are some thirty fishermen–they may each gain twenty pounds. The merchant, to gain a thousand, has risked a capital of perhaps two thousand. The sealer, to gain twenty, has risked his all–his life. If the voyage fails, the owner still has his ship, but the poor man returns with the loss of his labour and his time, penniless. If the vessel founder or be dashed to pieces in the ice, insurance relieves the merchant, but if thirty lives are lost, then

31

thirty widows and perhaps a hundred orphans shriek their curses on a fishery that gave them no compensation and was the grave of all their hopes....

Upon the successful return of a vessel, one-half of the proceeds is handed over to the owner; the other half divided amongst the men whose toil and daring produced it. But the merchant's half is clear, while the poor man's half is clipped. He is obliged to pay hospital dues and is taxed by the merchant to pay not only for the tools and materials used in the fishery, but a further sum of £3/10 Berth Money for the privilege of being allowed to hazard his life to secure a fortune for the merchant.

By about 1860 the pattern of the seal fishery as an organized exploitation of both men and seals had become firmly established. It was not to change significantly until the sealing game was finally played out. Yet here and there, in the most isolated of the northern settlements, a very few men continued to play it by the old, simple rules up to the very end, thereby providing a living memory of the way it used to be in the time of my forebears.

They says our great-great-grandfather was the first Budgel come to Cottrells Cove, and he settled there because of the swiles. Nets was the thing in them early times and wonderful big nets they was. But a good many of them old people would rather go gunning. They'd go off in rodneys–four-oared open boats–in January and February before the field ice filled up Notre Dame Bay entirely. They was after the old swiles, the big old harps, but was always glad for a try at the two-year-olds, the bedlamers, for they was best in the pot. They had them old Poole guns, as some calls them, swile guns eight feet long and firing a charge would kick you clean out of the boat if you didn't mind.

Later times they took to using bigger boats with a lugsail as well as oars. They'd go right into the ice with them boats, March-month when the swiles was whelping; but mainly they went swatching–shooting the old swiles on the edge of the ice and in the leads.

Two hundred year and more, I suppose, Budgels has swiled hereabouts. Me brother and me, we'm still at it, and just about the last to give it a lick. The spring of 1962 they was a good patch of whitecoats not forty mile off Cape St. John. Heard the ships talking about it on the ship-to-shore radio. So we set off in our twenty-eight-foot trapboat–wide open she was, except for a bit of a cuddy in the head, but good power into her. They was lots of loose ice but nary a swile until we got near the Grey Islands, and then the wind come easterly and the ice got so tight we had to haul the boat out onto it. And blow! She blew a living starm for five days. We was snug enough on the ice. Had a little ile stove to bile up the kettle. Course, it warn't exactly like being home....

Ten days we drifted. At last the wind come westerly again and the ice opened, but we daren't put the boat into it. 'Twas all broke up. She'd have been chewed to pieces like a crackie dog chews up a bone. Ten days, and we reckoned we'd drifted eighty mile or more afore the ice got good and open. Then we launched off, and bejasus if we didn't strike into old swiles. Leads was full of them. We spent the next two days swatching and filled her up. Put 206 sculps in that little boat, and she loaded down till every little slop come over her gunwales.

'Twas time to make for home. We cut a sou'west course till we raised Fogo Island light, and after that it was nothing but a pastime to run the forty miles back to the cove. The merchants in St. John's got nary smell of our fat. We trucked it to Port-aux-Basques, shipped it off to Halifax, and cleared $1,070.00. That's swilin', bye! That's the way to do her!

33

When my grandfather was a boy there were still a few people living on the Wadham Islands, although these were nothing more than a pile of bald-headed rocks, wide open to the Atlantic from the north and east. It was a terribly wild and lonely place but handy to the cod grounds as well as being right in the way of the old harp seals when they were coming south from Labrador.

The Wadham men were sealers first and cod fishermen second. They thought nothing at all of rowing miles offshore into the open ice in two-man punts, and sometimes they would get caught in a blow and be driven away. One spring three of the little boats were blown eastward in a sea of broken slob until they sighted the Funks, a desolate and dangerous rock heap forty miles out in the open ocean and the last land before you reach Iceland on a northeast course. The seas were breaking clean over the Funks, but the Wadham men knew they had to land or be swept away forever, and so they took the chance. Two of their boats were smashed to pieces, but all the men scrambled ashore and hauled the third boat to safety.

Three days later, when the wind dropped out, they piled all hands into the remaining boat and made for home, but a southeast blizzard caught them and they were adrift for two more days and nights and nearly perished from the cold. Although they were tremendously tough, no human flesh could stand that sort of thing, and they were close to giving it up when, during the second night, a great white bird, such as none of them had ever seen before, came out of the howling night and began circling their boat. It stayed with them until dawn and then flew off, mewling like a cat. They set their course after it and late that same day raised the Wadhams. The Wadham people were sure the bird was a sign sent to save their men, and as long as they continued to live on those islands none of them would ever shoot any white seabird.

Greenspond is a pretty place,
And so is Pinchards Island.
Me Ma will get a new silk dress
When Pa comes home from swilin'.

In my time people still told the story of the Wadham "sign," but *it* was a tale with a happy ending. Many other stories about the inshore sealers end in stark tragedy. Few of these have been recorded in Newfoundland's written history, but the Trinity Bay disaster is an exception.

«The morning of Saturday, 28th of February, 1892, ushered in a lovely dawn. A soft, bright, balmy air blew from the land over the treacherous ice fields. Small boats were out by early dawn, gunning for seals, which had been seen in numbers the previous evening. From Trinity, Ship Cove, Trouty, English Harbour, Salmon Cove, and many other small places the daring ice-hunters set off with high hopes to chase the wary seal. In this most exciting and daring of pursuits the Newfoundlander recks not of danger. Difficulties and perils that would afright one not accustomed to the ice fields are mere sport to the hardy native.

On this day seals were few and scattered. In the fierce excitement of the chase many boats rowed far out into the bay heedless of the signs of a coming tempest. A few of the older fishermen, more wary and perhaps less vigorous, noticed the first signs of storm and before the icy blast came down full force they gained the lee of the land and could row in.

Two hundred and fifteen men were out that day. Many got safe to land only after many hours of tremendous struggle, but the rest, in spite of their heroic efforts, were finally overpowered. The freezing ice tornado swept down upon them and paralyzed their efforts. One bold crew from English Harbour, seeing that all their attempts against the blizzard were in vain, made for the fields of ice. They managed to climb on a pan higher than the rest, where they made a rude shelter out of ice hummocks. Their boat was broken up to make a fire and with this and some seals they managed to live through the awful night.

Thirteen fishermen were found frozen to death in their little punts. Eleven others were driven up the bay and perished in the bitter dark. The agony of suspense for the dear ones on shore and the sufferings of those poor humble souls in their hour of agony is known only to the Almighty Power who rules the raging of the seas.»

— Adapted from History of Newfoundland
by D. W. Prowse

It was the men from the offer islands who were the great seal swatchers in small boats, but it was those from the inner coves, deep in the bays where good timber could be found, who brought the schooner seal fishery into being and who built it into the burgeoning but risky enterprise it had become by the mid-1800's.

Job Brothers,   3rd April. 1862.
St. John's   At Sea.

Sirs:

I regret that I cannot write to you so encouragingly as I would wish.

After leaving St. John's on the 12th of March I succeeded in getting out through all the ice and kept beating to windward until the 17th evening after I left. When I was 3 miles north of Partridge Point in Green Bay in consort with the Margaret we entered the ice with a heavy breeze of wind from N.N.E. to E.N.E. and a tremendous sea running. Both our ships were leaking and our pumps have been going ever since.

As for seals, I have 430 old Hoods and 460 young Hoods.

As to losses of ships, I am afraid the number will be fearful. I have seen six or eight go down the last few days among which are the Emily Tobin, the Melrose and the Margaret, besides several others I cannot name.

While I am writing there is so much sea, and the ice is so heavy, I cannot tell the moment the sides of my own vessel will be driven in. Since the 20th of March I have drifted from the Funks and we are now off Cape St. Francis and expect to drive to Cape Race before getting clear of the ice. I have Captain Cummins and crew on board since Sunday when they lost the Margaret.

I am yours, sirs, respectfully,
Edward White, Captain

The Manse,
St. Albans Church,
May 12th, 1872.

My Dearest Sister:

A heavy sorrow has fallen on us for the loss of the brig Huntsman, *120 tons burthen, owned and commanded by Captain Robert Dawe, with a crew of sixty-two. She was wrecked off the coast of Labrador on the night of April 28th while prosecuting the sealing; and therebye was lost her Master and his second son, with forty-one of the crew. The survivors were brought in aboard the brig* Rescue, *Captain Samuel Dawe, from whom we learned particulars of this dreadful event.*

On the morning of the 28th, in the vicinity of Cape Charles, a heavy gale with rain sprang up from the northeast which forced both the Rescue *and the* Huntsman, *who were in company, to seek shelter in the ice. They had not long entered it, and were tightly encompassed when they found it was running very fast in the grip of the tide and was likely to take their ships over some very shoal and dangerous ground. Nevertheless, they did not anticipate danger to life since the land was not far off and the ice lay thick and solid between them and the shore. The wind, however, increased and there was a heavy swell in the ice, and incessant rain, so that the night closed in very dark and gloomy. Yet they still hoped to drift clear of the shoals. They saw no sign of breakers until these were so close they could neither avoid them nor dared they then abandon their vessels.*

Suddenly a reef broke directly under the bow of the Huntsman *sending up such a tremendous sea that the ship was thrown on her beam ends and shattered against the rock, which stood just below the surface.*

The Rescue *was so close that her bowsprit almost overhung the ill-fated vessel. Her crew saw the huge wave rise, heard the shrieks of the poor fellows and the crash of timbers. Some of the* Huntsman's *crew leapt overboard and were at once crushed or drowned. Most of them, however, took refuge in the rigging. Their Captain was seen from the* Rescue *clinging to the halyards. Twice he was swung far out over the ice and back to the stricken ship. The* Huntsman *then took a final roll and the masts went out of her with a terrible crash and those who had taken refuge in the rigging were flung upon the churning ice where, sad to relate, most of them perished. Only eighteen were rescued and, of these, all but three of the poor fellows were grievously injured from breaking their legs and arms with their fall upon the ice. None of them can tell how they got to safety at all.*

When this dreadful news reached us I caused the church bell to be rung and although it was but Monday morning, many were the sorrowing men and women who came to me seeking some comfort in their terrible affliction. We remain in the deepest distress and hardly know how our small village shall bear the loss which has been laid upon us....

*"When Mr. Walter Grieve sent the first steamer to the ice,
it was a poor day for Newfoundland."*

The first sixty years of going to the whelping ice belonged to sail
and to the outport settlements, but that began to change when, in the spring
of 1862, the sealers at the ice were astounded to see billowing black plumes of
smoke appear on the horizon. These signalled the beginning of a new age for
our people – the coming of steam, and the death knell to sail. The smoke
came from two Scots steam-auxiliary whalers taking a look at sealing possi-
bilities before proceeding on their annual voyage for whales in Davis Strait.

The *Polynia* and the *Camperdown* could hardly have chosen a worse
spring to try their luck. Ice conditions were awesome. A succession of nor'-
easters had raftered the arctic pack so heavily that the whole sailing fleet was
jammed and scores of ships were crushed and lost. The two auxiliary whalers,
clipper-bowed and high-masted, belching clouds of coal smoke from their
tall, narrow stacks, butted their way into the pack but took such a pummel-
ling they had to withdraw – without having killed a single seal between them.
That year it was "landsmen's luck" and the whole population of the Green
Bay settlements had gone out over the floes from shore to make the largest
kill of whitecoats ever taken from the land.

In May the two steamers continued north about their whaling business and it seemed that their *future* business would not include sealing. However, there was one St. John's merchant prince-in-the-making, Walter Grieve,
who was very thoughtful after the whalers left. True, they had taken no
seals, but their performance in the ice, even with tiny steam engines rated at
a mere 60 horsepower, had seemed almost miraculous compared with what
vessels under sail alone could do.

Walter Grieve did more than think. He sent an agent off to Dundee
and bought the little S.S. *Wolf*, 200 tons, powered by a 30-horsepower auxiliary engine. The bustling St. John's firm of Baine, Johnson and Company
got wind of the move and bought a steamer too, the 40-horsepower S.S.
Bloodhound.

Between them, the two little wooden steamers brought in 4,300 seals
in 1863. It was a small enough showing but it sparked a rush by St. John's
merchant firms to buy up any sea-weary steam-auxiliary whalers they could
find. Within ten years twenty-six old whalers had been purchased and in
1873 twenty-two of them brought back 300,000 sculps. The other four
steamers had been lost at the ice. The *Bloodhound* and the *Wolf* were both
gone – the *Bloodhound* in 1872 in an incident which was a clear enough
indication that, efficient as they might be, the new ships could be almost as
vulnerable as their sailing predecessors had been.

*...The steamers were caught in the same storm with the brig Hunts-
man and, in the dark of the night, the Bloodhound struck, or was flung
upon, an island of ice and was so much damaged that it was only by
the greatest efforts her crew were enabled to keep her afloat until dawn,
half an hour after which she suddenly went down. Marooned upon the
moving ice, her crew spied the S.S. Retriever jammed in the pack about*

two miles away, and they made haste toward her. Imagine their feelings when, upon arriving alongside, they found that she too had been shattered by the ice and was fast sinking. There was then nothing for it but for all the men, numbering more than three hundred, to try and make their way over the shifting ice to the distant, rocky shore of Labrador. That they were enabled to do this without great loss of life can only be attributed to the Grace of the Lord.

On reaching the coast they struggled along it to Battle Harbour where the few poor inhabitants did what they could for the destitute sealers. Presently they were joined by the crews of two large sailing vessels, which also had been crushed while pursuing the elusive seal. These distressed men then endured great hardships for some days, being in want of food, clothing, shelter, and other necessities, until some of the men spied the S.S. Nimrod at a distance. They tried to attract her attention by making signals. When that failed, our sealers, who are not easily discouraged, finding an ancient and rusty cannon lying on a hill, filled it with a tremendous charge of powder and applied the match. The explosion blew the cannon into a thousand pieces, but those on the Nimrod saw the flash or heard the concussion and drew near enough to send men in over the ice.

I t was the Scots who first put steam power into the whaling ships and from the first the steam-auxiliaries built in Dundee were a great success. They were built so strong they were nearly as solid as an ironwood log; but there was precious little space left in them for men. It was hard lines for the whaling crews. Thirty or forty whalers would be packed into one of those small ships like birds in a barrel, but they had luxury accommodations compared to what our fellows got when the whaling ships were bought up by the St. John's merchants for the sealing game. The new owners thought nothing of jamming as many as *two hundred* men into each ship, and keeping them there for weeks on end.

To save on coal, and to increase their power, the whalers were all ship-rigged and, to tell the truth, could often make better speed under a full spread of canvas than under steam power. It was said of the little S.S. *Kite* that whenever she blew her whistle she would come to a dead stop, not having steam enough for whistle and engine both. Still, it was steam power that made these ships cunning in the ice.

Their strength, and the way they could take punishment, was hard to believe. Some of those built in the early 1870's were still afloat, still battling the ice, in the late 1930's. They were such wonderful ice ships that arctic and antarctic expeditions setting out as late as the 1920's still chose the old "wooden walls," as they became known, in preference to modern steel vessels. The wooden sealer S.S. *Terra Nova*, built in 1885, carried Captain Robert Scott's ill-fated party to the antarctic in 1910. She was one of the last wooden walls ever built, and one of the most powerful:

One hundred and eighty-six feet long, her tonnage is 450, and her engine is of 120 H.P....Oak, ironbark, and greenheart are the principal woods used...her bows are protected by a very heavy stem strengthened with iron ice plates, and the bolts securing the stem plates pass through about ten feet of solid wood...the fortifications in the bows consist of huge oak diagonals, two feet in cross section, and two tiers of ice beams almost as heavy extending backward a distance of fifty feet. The planking throughout is over two feet thick.

By the time the *Terra Nova* was launched, the arctic whaling game was practically played out. The bowheads were nearly finished and the battered old steam whalers were not wanted anymore in Scotland, so they were bought up for a song by the St. John's merchants. Steam took over at the ice almost completely and, as a result, the St. John's merchants – the Pirates of Water Street, as many of our people called them – took over the whole sealing business, and the settlements where it had all started were cut out. There was only one thing left for our men to do – work for the St. John's owners aboard the steamers under conditions that were just a bit better than slavery. It was a great time for the Water Street crowd. A good many of them became millionaires, and it seemed they didn't much care how they made their millions. Right from the first, the way they ran the ships was nothing short of criminal.

They was the finest kind of ships, when they was built. Aye, there was none better on the sea. But they got no care from the owners and when they went to the ice some of the skippers used to bate them up something terrible. 'Twas a wonder any of them ever did come back...yet back they come, year after year, some of them for as long as a man's lifetime...I've seen them come in through the Notch at St. John's so log-loaded the water was sluicing over their decks and them leaking so bad all hands was at the pumps or bailing the water out with buckets. They never had no load lines. Some skippers would fill them to the hatches, then put near as many sculps again on deck. Oftentimes they'd start home from the ice, get into the smallest little starm, and have to run back into the ice for shelter, or down they would have gone – they were that overloaded. One time Captain Edward White brought the Neptune in with 32,000 seals on deck and below, and another 6,000 towing on a cable off her quarter! Her second hand told I: "If an ice-bird had squirted onto we, we'd have gone down like a stone!" Aye, 'twas cruel the way them ships was treated, and cruel the way the men was treated too...but what fine names they had! Panther, Tigress, Nimrod, and Esquimaux...Proteus, Hector, Lion, and Eagle...Polynia, Viking, and Aurora...Falcon, Hope, and Ariel...'twas as good as music just to say them over to yourself....

With Harvey's I'll start and to Bowrings I'll go,
And I'll name all the ships and the captains also.
When the North King is raging and strong blows the gale,
In search of the whitecoats, today they will sail.
In the Ad, Captain Doyle; in the Belle, Joby Knee;
In the Bon, Captain Parsons—a stout man is he.
And Skipper Wes Kean this spring will command
Harvey's fine steamer, the old Newfoundland.
The good ship Diana, Joe Blandford has charge,
And I hopes she'll come back before long with a surge.
Out goes the Beothic, so swift and so sure,
I guess that Joe Barbour is with her once more.
And there goes the Neptune, bound for the ice plain,
And likewise the Eric, with pleasant Joe Kean.
There's the Bloodhound, Nate Winsor, he'll sure make his mark;
William Kean in the Iceland; and the Cross, Captain Clarke.
The Kite, Captain Carrol, I wish him good luck.
And out in the Eagle Job Kean shows his pluck.
And Bartlett, the Viking I hope you will fill.
Dan Green in the Thetis, may he make a big bill.
The Ranger, Sam Winsor, be fleetingly seen,
Likewise Noah Bishop in the Algerine.

So my song is concluded, 'bout captains and ships.
And may they come home with big beards on their lips!

    —Sealers' song, c. 1910

If the ships were famous, their skippers were even more so, for they became the supreme folk heroes of Newfoundland. My father sailed with many of them before he got his own command, and he would talk about them as if they had been members of his own family.

On the first off, the steamer skippers were mostly Scotsmen, captains of the Dundee whalers as brought their ships into St. John's in the spring of the year to take up a crew of our sealers. That was afore our skippers got the hang of them new kind of ships. The Scotsmen was the finest kind and they taught our skippers a good deal. There was the Adamses, father and son; Jimmie Bannerman; Jim Fairweather and his brother Alex, and that famous chappie William Guy.

However, 'twarn't long afore our own skippers took hold of the steamers, and when they did, my dear man, didn't they make the seal scutters* fly! Early times, most of the skipper-men hailed from along the southern shore or from Trinity and Conception Bays, but 'twarn't long afore we northern bay men come to the top. As the sailing ships went out and the steamers come in, there was twenty skipper-men for every ship, and didn't they fight for to get hold of a command! That was a fine thing for the owners. They could take their pick, and if a skipper didn't come in top dog, why out he'd go, for there was plenty begging to take his place. The competition was good for the catch but hard on the ships and hard on the men.

The biggest part of the skipper-men run in families. There was four Blackwoods, four Jackmans, four Blandfords, five Winsors, seven Dawes, eight Barbours, ten Keans, and ten Bartletts. Mostly they come into steam without any foolishness about master's certificates. A good many of them had no learning and some couldn't read or write. The most of them was no great hands at deep-sea navigating, either. Old Captain Peter Mullowney, talking about his ship, used to say: "Me sons, I don't know where this one's at and I don't care, for by the Lard Jasus, I knows where the swiles is to, and I can find 'em in me sleep!"

They was a powerful hardy lot. Had to be. And they was God so far as the men was concerned. A skipper might go in charge of the same ship twenty springs to the ice, and likely the most of his men would stay with him, for they was as staunch to a good skipper as they was to the King in London. To call another man's skipper down was always good for a row.

William Bartlett, who belonged to Brigus, went forty-two springs to the ice as master. He was a jowler true enough...a skipper as got the seals; would bring his ship home log-loaded and a big pay bill for every man aboard. Sam Blandford was another, a proper wildman he was—would pound a man one minute and give him his shirt the next, but no better fellow ever went to the ice.

The one I remembers best was Skipper Henry Dawe. Now there was a swiler! Went to the ice as a common hand in 1863 and by 1875 was a skipper-man and the finest kind. I went with him in 1914 in the Ranger, the year of the big disasters, and that was his fifty-first spring to the ice, but he never lost a man in all his time. Lost plenty of seals because he wouldn't put his men to the risk, and always watched the barometer and kept an eye on the weather.

*The webbed, compressed hind feet with which seals swim are called scutters.

Too bad they warn't all the like of Skipper Henry. I supposes Captain Abraham Kean was top dog for the number of seals. Forty-four trips to the ice, and he brought back a million sculps. My, my, my, what a swile killer that man was! 'Course, some says he was a man killer too. Fair crazy to get the seals, he was, and never a one to worry overmuch what happened to his men.

They was a quare lot, certainly. Some used to burn down in the ice – drop the steam pressure to save coal – at midnight on a Saturday and every man aboard would have to go to prayer meeting next day even supposing they was in the middle of the whelping ice and it fair crawling with whitecoats waiting to be sculped. Then they was others would spend Sunday cruising the floes, stealing the panned pelts other ships had left behind to pick up at a later time. They was some as took the men's condition to heart and more that wouldn't give them a thought. Some as would sooner lose a man than a seal. A quare lot, indeed they was, but proper men for all o' that. 'Tisn't likely we'll see the like of them again.

Skipper Ned Bishop were a gert pillar of the Church.
'Twas more'n you was worth to bring a drop of rum
aboard his ship. He was a hardy man as only spoke
to we on Sunday when he led us in the prayers.
When we was in the ice he almost never left the bridge.
There was just one thing in his head—to get the fat!
Find where the main patch lay and load the Eagle up.
If seals was scarce, he'd stay at sea until hell froze.
When all the coal was burned, he'd make we hist the sails;
and when the grub run out, he'd make we dine on swiles!

I mind one loo'ard spring the whole fleet missed the patch.
Most of the vessels give it up and come home clean.
Not Skipper Ned! We stayed out nine tormenting weeks;
cruising the ice-edge till all hands was wore to death.
'Twas more and flesh and blood could bear, so I was chose
to tell the Old Man that we'd work the ice no more.

He and his officers was on the bridge when I come aft.
They heered my footsteps on the ladder; turned their heads.
The Old Man spun around. He knowed why I was there!
His eyes was harder than the ice. "Captain," I says,
"we'd best heave up and cut for home. We's all bate out..."
And then me throat went dry. He only stood and glared
until I guessed I'd hang there till me eyeballs froze.

At last he roared: "Go forward now, me son, and tell the men
what Captain Neddy said:
Before I takes me orders from a slinjing lot like you,
we'll all be damned well dead!"

The traditional date for the departure of the sailing fleet had originally been March 1st, but with the coming of steam the new ships were able to reach the whelping ice so quickly that the newborn seals – "cats," they were called – were still too small and thin to be of much value. It was not until their mothers had nursed them for at least a week that they became layered with the thick coating of fat that was the sealer's prize. However, rather than let some other ship get them, the steam sealers would kill the very young and almost worthless whitecoats anyway. Finally the owners agreed to postpone the departure day for steamers to March 10th.

As that day drew near, the steamer skippers forgathered in St. John's, where they prowled around each other like suspicious mastiffs. Soon enough each of them would be trying to cut out his fellows, to find the main patch of seals without being followed, to get his men on ice before anyone else; if he had bad luck, to steal the fat killed and panned by more successful men; and finally, to come home first, log-loaded, to the plaudits of the St. John's population.

But that was for the future. In the last few days before sailing, these hopeful jowlers at least pretended to be boon companions, since they were, after all, the most famous men in our island, and a class apart.

So they would gather to have a "time" together, and then these men, who would soon be competing ferociously for seals, engaged in competition of another sort as each captain sought to out-drink, out-sing, and out-dance his peers.

As I leaned o'er the rail of the Eagle
A letter-boy brought unto me
A little gilt-edged invitation,
Saying the girls wants you over for tea.
Sure, I knew 'twas Sam Blandford as sent it,
But I went just for old friendship sake,
And the first thing they give me to tackle
Was a slice of that Trinity cake!

'Twas baked up with flutes and mouth organs,
And handles of double-edged files.
Covers of clergymen's forgers,
And pieces of broken bass viols.
Blue lights and petticoat jumpers
That would build up a fine stomachache,
For 'twould kill a man twice after eating a slice
Of that wonderful Trinity cake!

Two sealers attacked it with handspikes
To try to remove the top crust,
While McCarthy went out for a hatchet
And Flannigan grabbed an old saw.
For that cake was enough, by the Powers,
To paralyze any man's jaw.

There was glass-eyes, bull's-eyes, and stale butter,
Lampwicks and liniment too.
Pastry as hard as a shutter
That a billy goat's jaws couldn't chew.
Tobacco and whiskers of crackies
That would give you the fever and ache.
You'd crack off at the knees if you happened to sneeze,
After eating that Trinity cake.

– Traditional song from Trinity Bay

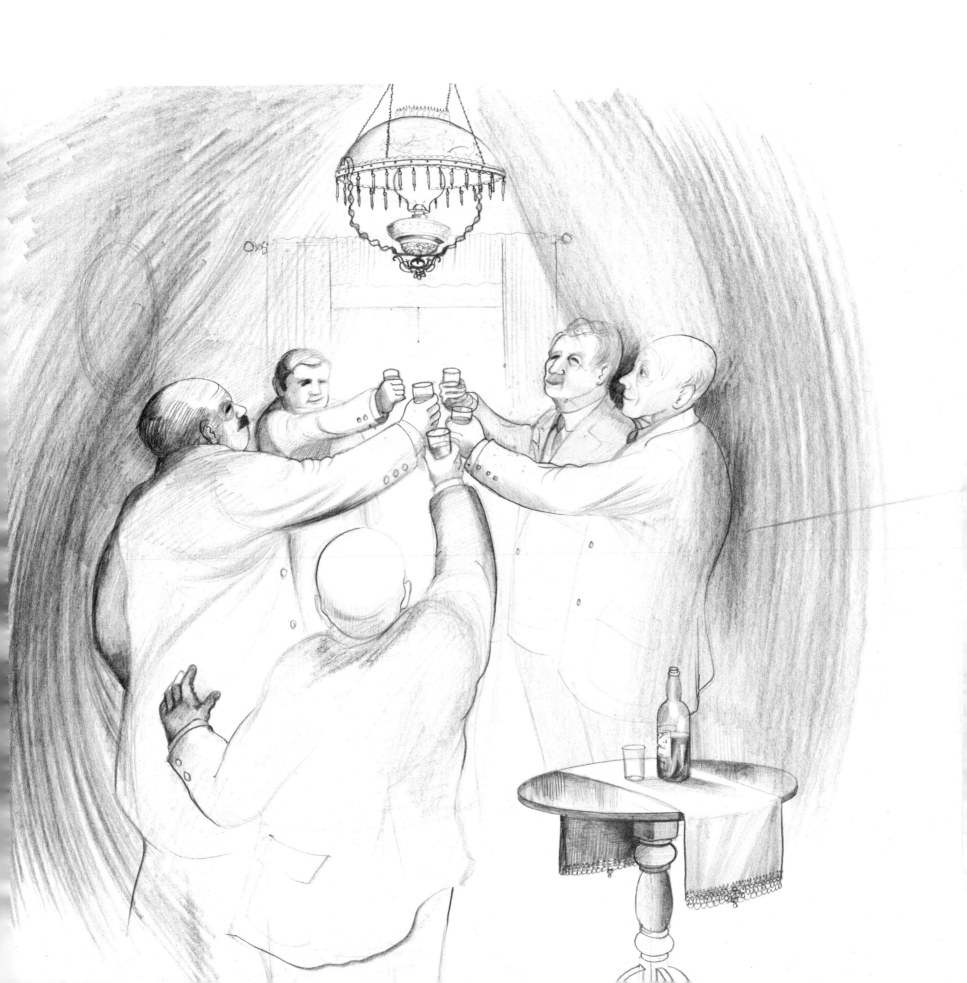

W hile the wooden walls lay at their owners' wharves in St. John's harbour, taking aboard their niggardly allocation of provisions, coal, and other supplies, and while the captains enjoyed their times ashore, multitudes of men from distant outports would be converging on the capital city.

The roads begin to be enlivened by the appearance of the swilers, each with his bundle of spare clothing on his shoulder. This light wardrobe he carries on a stick six or eight feet long, which is called a gaff; it has a hooked iron head and serves also as a bat to strike the seals on the nose, as an ice pole in leaping from pan to pan, and as a tool for dragging the skin of the seal over the fields and hummocks of ice to the side of the vessel. Some of the men, in addition, carry a long sealing gun. These men rank before batsmen, or common sealers, being the gunners who will kill old seals after the whitecoats have been harvested...The outfit of the sealers is of the simplest description: sealskin boots, called skinnywoppers, that reach to the knees and have a thick leather sole, well nailed with sparrables or frosters to enable them to walk over the ice; coarse canvas or cotton jackets, often showing the industry of wife or mother in the number of patches that adorn them, which are worn over an undershirt; and sealskin caps and moleskin trousers – the reverse of handsome or picturesque.

T hus, an account written by a well-bred St. John's townsman about 1870, as if he were describing an invasion by a crowd of rather unsavoury savages, and this is how the "townies" *did* regard the outport sealers.

The point of view of the sealers themselves was somewhat different, as my father's old shipmate, Captain Llewelyn Kean of Greenspond, described it.

In 1910, when I was just turned sixteen, I made up my mind it was time to make my first trip to the ice. Right after Christmas I began looking for a berth, but it was near as hard to get a berth-ticket as an invitation to the Governor's Ball in St. John's. Times was hard and there was only about fifteen steamers going sealing that year, carrying from a hundred and fifty up to two hundred and fifty men aboard of each; and for every berth-ticket there was three men wanted it. You'd wonder at that, sure. The food was so bad, so wonderful scarce, it would hardly have kept a crackie dog alive...two men or more in every bunk, jammed down in the hold among the pens of coal, and bare boards for your mattress...no heat, barring a little bogey stove that would hardly bile a kettle; and an oil lantern to light a hundred men. Dirty, dark, and cold it was, and the slaving out on the ice would nearly take your life away. The pay bill was next to nothing. When you did get aboard you took your crop from the owner—a sheath knife, snow goggles of celluloid, and a bag of raisins and oatmeal. Together it was worth maybe three or four dollars, but you got cropped twelve dollars for it from your share of the seal fat. The way the shares was worked was different from the sailing days when there was a small crew of men, and they got half the value of the voyage. On the steamers there was always a terrible big crowd, but the owner took two-thirds of the voyage, leaving only a third for all them men to share. You were some lucky if you cleared thirty dollars after your crop was took out, and that for six or seven weeks of the devil's own work.

Didn't seem to matter. A berth to the ice was what you had to have, supposing you had to lie down and beg for it. Only a few years back, a man had to pay for his berth. When Job Brothers brought the old Neptune over from Dundee, she paid for herself in fifteen years from berth money alone! In my time the owners would give out tickets for half the berths and the captain give out the other half. You'd stand no chance to get one unless you as much as guaranteed to sell all your fish to, and buy all your year's grub and gear from, that merchant or his outport dealer.

But still you had to go. Oft-times I asks myself why we was so foolish. Perhaps it was like going off to the wars. Certainly there was risk enough and blood enough. It seemed like you weren't a proper man at all unless you'd gone to the ice and, of course, when you'd gone once, odds was you'd keep on with it until you was froze to death sometime or was getting too well-up to stand the gaff.

Anyway, it was the number one excitement of the year, and there was the gamble that kept you at it. Always the chance your ship would make a bumper voyage, fill to the hatches, and every man would bring home a big bill. But it was a poor sort of gamble because the merchants set the price for the fat, and if it was a good year at the ice, they'd drop the price of fat down to nothing at all.

I got my ticket, on the last of it, from Skipper Jobie Kean who was my mother's brother. We was to join our ships in St. John's by the fifth of March. The first day of March there was four hundred and more men from all along the nor'western shore of Bonavista Bay ready to get under way. That was a sight to see! We started off before dawn from Wesleyville, bound for Gambo about sixty mile away over frozen ponds, through the woods, over the barrens, and across frozen bays. There was no roads them times, so it was all shanks' mare. Some fellows carried their bags on their shoulders but more pulled them on little wooden slides. There was some made it straight through, never stopping except to bile the kettle now and again. Others used to hang up in Hare Bay the first night and go on again in the morning.

When that great string of men started across Dark Cove to Lower Gambo, all the local youngsters would be waiting. They'd run out on the ice and take the slides and haul them to the railroad station. They kept the slides for their pay.

Men come into Gambo from all sides. I've seen close to a thousand sealers jamming the town, and no place to sleep except in the cars on the siding. They had special cars for sealers—the oldest, dirtiest they could find. We never cared about that. It might be two, three days before the train pulled out for St. John's, but every man had his own grub, and it was a grand enjoyment to be along of that big crowd. A scattered fellow would get drunk, and a scattered one might start a row. Great fun it was for all of we young fellows.

We youngsters never slept the night before they sailed.
Not many people did. It was the milestone of the year.
The fleet was going to the ice! Long before dawn
the docks and hills were skeined and clotted dark
with people drawn to the harbour side from miles around.
The bleak March sky was threaded with great veins of smoke
as the old ships stoked up to get the biggest head of steam
their worn old boilers could withstand. At each gangplank
the master watches stood; close-written crew lists in their hands
to check off every man who'd had the luck to get a berth.
Wild laughter and great shouts of merriment rang out
so loud you would have thought this was the greatest day
in all our history. A celebration of unrivalled joy
and vast excitement. So it was . . . and yet, the voyage ahead,
fate-freighted for the ice, might bring them death,
disfigurement – was sure to be a time of hardships that you'd think
only demented souls would voluntarily embrace.

Aboard the ancient, grimy ships they searched for stowaways;
youngsters who were so drunkenly enthralled
by the cold fire of the ice they'd risk their unlived lives,
struggle and curse like savages when they were caught
and hove ashore. At fourteen years of age I stowed away
aboard the *Imogene*. Hid in the scunner's barrel on her mast.
The lines were loosed before the master watch swarmed up
the shrouds . . . and drove me out of it. At eight they sailed.
The cheers rang back from ship to ship, from ship to shore
and, from the cliffs, old muzzle-loading guns blew out
black puffs of smoke and roared like God. The rusty blast
of the ships' whistles raised plumed serpents of white steam.
. . . Old die-hard ships! Yet so majestic. Out they swept.
And, left behind, I hid myself and wept.

Fifty years going to the ice! It should have been enough
for any man. It would have been for most, but Skipper Alph
was born with seal's blood running through his veins.
When the hard northern ice swelled south toward the Funks,
and Paddy's Brush brought in the first spring gale,
not wife, nor devil, could have held him to his home.
A proper jowler, Skipper Alpheus was. Year after year
the same crowd came to him for berths aboard the old *Neptune*.
Long faces then, the spring when word went round
that Skipper Alph was sick. He'd found his heart;
could scarcely breathe; lay white-faced in his bed
in his big house upon the hill. The doctor shook his head
when sealers stopped him on the road and asked the news.

The *Neptune* fitted at St. John's that spring, though no one knew
who'd take command. Her owners sent up word to Skipper Alph,
asked who he'd recommend. The Old Man's answer was:
"Let her come on to Wesleyville. I'll find your man."
On March the 10th that good old wooden wall steamed down the bay.
Her barricade was lined with men, all wondering
who the Old Man would choose. Agape, they watched the shore
where a trap boat was putting out, pounding her way
into a steep head-sea. A whisper started . . . mounted to a roar!
"By the Lard Livin' Jasus, byes, 'tis him! 'Tis Skipper Alph!"
And so it was; they hoisted him aboard strapped to a chair.
Gentle as women, carried him below where, from his berth,
through five long weeks out in the ice he held to his command,
then brought the *Neptune* home, log-loaded, to the land!

Small wonder that our sealers loved the man.

Next to the captains of the sealing ships – Olympian figures, closely linked to the owners and almost as untouchable – came the master watches. There were four of them aboard each steamer and the entire crowd of sealers was divided equally among them into four watches. On ice the master watch was as much in command of his thirty to fifty men as if he had been the master of a vessel and they his crew. However, since he was not possessed of the magic cloak of authority which enfolded the actual ships' officers, he had to reach and maintain his position by being superlatively good in everything he did – and this among a crowd of men who vied desperately with one another to kill the most seals, copy on the worst ice, drag the heaviest tows of sculps, venture farthest from the ships, take the greatest risks, and endure the worst hardships. A master watch had need to be a veritable Titan.

He also had to be a man who could bear a terrifying responsibility. While the captain was responsible for the safety of the men as long as they were aboard the ship, and for finding them and picking them up once they had gone out on the ice, it was the master watch in whose hands their lives lay while they were away from the vessel. And it was away from the ship, far out on the ice, that the most deadly perils lay.

The master watches were truly men of heroic stature, and it is because of them that the roster of human victims of the seal fishery is not infinitely greater. It was little wonder that, while great captains were worshipped from afar, it was the master watches who became the living legends of outport Newfoundland.

Five thousand men of the island breed will sail for the ice today.
An eager throng fills the city streets and, loud from the crowded quay,
The answering cheer to the shrill of horns proclaims where the ships do lay.

But back in a dingy street there lies, enfeebled and faint and poor,
All grizzled and grey, a dying man whose sealing days are o'er.
The master watch, of the fearless heart, will tread the pans no more.

Oh, eager, alert, and brave was he, and fleet of foot as the doe.
Through nights of stress he's cheered his men when lost on the running floe,
And his eagle eye was the first to sight his ship through the whirling snow.

"Ah yes, I can hear them cheering now – they're off to the ice today.
And I was with them fifty year, and I knows where the whitecoats play.
I knows where the main patch drifting goes and the seals in thousands lay.

"I've led my men where the harps abound, and the hunters' cheering rings.
Today they sail, and I cannot go, yet memory fondly sings.
And my heart is away upon the floe where the bloodstained batten swings."

– Sealers' song

There's a noble fleet of sealers being fitted for the ice.
They'll take a chance again this year, though fat's gone down in price.
The ice is drifting suddard, 'tis getting near the Funks,
So men will leave their featherbeds to sleep on wooden bunks.
Though times is getting hard again, our men has not gone soft.
They'll haul their tows o'er icy floes and briskly go aloft.

The Imogene is first to sail, she's steaming out the harbour
With eager sealers on her decks, and on the bridge, Wilf Barbour.
The northern blood runs in his veins as in the days of yore
When Barbours fished the seal and whale, and fished the Labrador.

The Ranger was the last to sail, but first to strike the patches;
On March the twenty-ninth bore up, log-loaded to the hatches.
They'll soon be back in old St. John's, a-sharing out the flippers.
So here's good luck to sealers all, likewise their gallant skippers.
Though Newfoundland be changing fast, some things we'll never lose.
We'll always have our flipper pie, likewise our fish and brews.

    —Sealers' song, c. 1930

Jacob Kelloway, who belonged to Greenspond and was a close chum of my father's, having sailed with him many times to the ice, was a master watch for thirty-seven springs. He was also a great storyteller, and he remembered what seemed like every last detail of his long life as a sealer. He never tired of telling us his history, and we youngsters never tired of listening.

The steamer fleet always made a grand display, hightailing nor'ard along the coast from St. John's, making to round Cape St. Francis with all sail set and smoke a-pouring out of every stack. Aye, and every man aboard desperate anxious to get into the swiles. But there was never no telling where the whelping pans might lie—might be anywhere from off of Hawke Harbour on the Labrador, right away out to the Grand Banks, four hundred mile to the sou'east.

I remembers one time I shipped in the Adventure *with Captain Henry Dawe. There was eighteen steamers in the fleet that spring, and they was all mostly in sight of each other when we run through Baccalieu Tickle. But we was in the fore, and Skipper Henry hauled off for the Funks and when we took the ice that evening there was nar' sign of any other ship, only a smudge of smoke on the horizon, for they was all still holding to the land.*

Once into the ice it was every skipper for himself. Unlucky ones used to dog the better men, sometimes so close they'd come right aboard with their big bowsprits. That used to drive Captain Abe Kean right wild. One time when he was in the Terra Nova *he was dogged by the little* Kite, *and he undertook to put a stop to that by running the* Terra Nova *into a field of old arctic ice, the thick blue sort as is as hard as iron. He calculated the* Kite *would get jammed and he could leave her far behind. But 'twas the* Terra Nova *got jammed herself. Kean couldn't free her, even with dynamite, for three days and nights. When the* Kite's *skipper saw what was up he backed her out of the hard ice, took a cut to the eastward, fell onto the main patch, loaded to the gunwales in them three days, and was the first ship back into St. John's.*

'Twas wonderful how news got around amongst the ships, even before they had the wireless. A vessel might look to be all alone in the world the day she struck the patches, but by next morning there'd likely be a half dozen ships butting into the floes all around her and putting their men on ice.

We struck a corner of the main patch late on March 14th, but before 'twas full dark the Terra Nova *hove in sight and hard in her wake come the* Ungava, Neptune, Thetis, *and* Beothic! *Skipper Henry was vexed to death, but there was nothing to be done.*

I don't say as any man slept much that night...all hands waiting for daybreak to get in among the whitecoats what was bawling every which way, all around the ships. When it come light we see the Terra Nova *so close on our starboard bow you could almost hear her smoke rushing overhead. All the ships was getting up steam and starting to put their men over the side. And what a wonderful sight it was—close to a thousand men spilling out onto the ice with their gaffs and their pan flags. 'Twas like some old-time army going off to war.*

If some sadistic prison commissioner had ever set out to design the ultimate hell-ship, he could hardly have done better than to take as his model one of the old wooden walls of the Newfoundland seal fishery. Any unfortunate prisoners sentenced to serve time in such a vessel would soon have been driven to riot or suicide. And yet every spring thousands of freeborn islanders would *volunteer*, and even fight for the *right*, to serve on these ships. Why they should have done so remains a mystery, for I never knew a sealer who could give a reasonable explanation. " 'Twas the excitement of it," some might say, if hard pressed. Or: " 'Twas a great lark for we bay fellows." It could hardly have been the money involved, for the men got precious little of that. Part of it may have been the need to stick to established tradition, and it had been traditional almost from the first that going to the ice entailed almost unimaginable hardships and dangers. Some "experts" have said the whole thing was akin to what anthropologists refer to among primitive tribes as the rites of passage, when youths earned the right to be called men by deliberately accepting physical agony and courting the possibility of death. That might help explain why youngsters *first* went to the ice; but how to explain why a man would continue to endure those agonies every spring of his life until he died of them or became too old to get a berth?

My grandfather went to the ice for nearly half a century, and though he was a captain for a good part of that time, he spent many years as a common sealer. He had no illusions about the life, and yet he returned to it, spring after spring. . . .

The first wooden wall as ever I shipped aboard was the S.S. Esquimaux. She was a little thing, only about a hundred feet overall, and had been a whaler for thirty year before being bought up for the sealing. She was soaked through and through with whale and seal oil and the stink of her was enough to make a goat lose his dinner. She was built with accommodation for maybe twenty men, but she carried a hundred and sixty the spring I went in her, and we was out ten weeks, most of it in the ice with northerly gales and the coldest kind of weather. I don't suppose I was dry half the time, for there was no place to dry out your clothes, supposing you dared take them off. We worked in the same clothes, lived in them, from the beginning to the end, and them soaked in seal fat and blood and dirt till they was so stiff they'd crackle. We slept in them too, for there was no such thing to be had as any sort of bedding. The only time I warn't chilled half to death was when we was on the ice working seals, and then you was on the go so hard you had to get warm.

As for the grub, 'twas hard to believe a man could live on it, let be work like a darkie slave. Five days a week it was nothing at all but hardtack and black tea. The hardtack–ship's biscuit, some calls it–was likely full of weevils and harder than ten-penny nails. The tea was made up in the morning by the galley-bitch–one of the sealers serving as the cook—in ten-gallon coppers. A handful of tea and a scoop of 'lasses was throwed into the water and left to boil away all day with more water added as the men drank it up. Water? I suppose you could call it that. The tanks on them old ships was so foul we mostly used water melted from ice we hauled aboard across the decks, sometimes knee-deep in seal sculps, blood, coal dust, and ashes. Twice a week, Tuesdays and Thursdays, we got duff, made out of condemned flour put into bags and boiled in a slut—a big kettle—with a bit of salt pork. The cook would sling them out, half-a-duff to a man, and you could manage to glutch them down while they was hot, but let them get cold and they was turned into cannon balls. Sundays we got a bit of salt fish to go with our hardtack. Small wonder most of us learned to eat raw sealmeat. The heart, when it was fresh cut out and still warm, was as good as steak to we fellows.

Some men brought along a bit of grub of their own. The crowd from Trinity Bay used to bring potatoes and eat them raw. Most of us had a little bag of oatmeal and another of raisins, but we kept that for when we was on the ice.

The queer thing about it was there was no complaints. The men took it all for nothing. Before we got into the patches you'd think they was having the finest kind of holiday. You never heard so much yarning and singing and carrying on in your life. Of course, once we got into the fat, all that went out. There was no time then for anything but work. Out to the ice you'd go before dawnlight, and you'd be on ice all of the day and maybe all the night too if the captain didn't happen to get back for you. When you did get back aboard, your supper was hardtack and black tea, and then you'd work on deck, icing and stowing down seal sculps maybe till midnight or later. Or you'd be shifting coal, carrying it in baskets to the stokehold or hauling ashes up on deck for the firemen. If there was plenty seals the bunks would be tore up to make pens for the fat 'tween decks, and the men would be crowded out and have to sleep on deck, supposing they had time to sleep. Many's the time I've laid down on a pile of steaming seal sculps. They was softer than them old plank bunks at any rate.

Things got a mite better after 1914, when William Coaker, the man as started the Fishermen's Union, made the government pass a law to improve the food. After that the men got dried pea soup twice a week. I remember Captain Abraham Kean was right wild about that. "Mark me!" I heard him say. "'Twill be the death of the sealing game. Too much luxury, that's what! Why, I remember when we never even had stoves aboard 'cause the owners thought the men would stay and warm theirselves 'stead of going on the ice...Now sealing's a pure luxury, with engines to do the work and bunks and hot food...it ain't a man's game any more!"

Skipper Abe was the hardest kind of a man, and maybe that was why he got so many seals. His men was right feared of him, aye, even his officers was. They'd do anything at all, take their lives in their hands day and night, rather than chance being called down for a hangback afore the rest of the crowd. A man had to keep up with the rest, put up with whatever was going, or he'd be ruined, certainly.

Aye, it was hard times, but if you lived through it, sure, you could look ary man in the face afterwards. And 'twasn't the hard times you remembered. What I recalls the best was the times we used to have 'tween decks when the ship was jammed or there was no seals about. Good times, me son. Aye, they was that.

Two jinkers in our harbour dwelt, all venturesome and plucky.
The plans they made all promised well—and always turned unlucky.
Misfortune followed on their trail wherever they did venture,
And when bad luck did us assail, those two we'd always censure.
To the fishing grounds, if they are bound—watch out for squalls that even!
"Make for the land," cries every man. "Here's Jimmie Walsh and Stephen."
Once when we landed on the Funks with them two Cat Cove ruffians,
They both went batting Carey's Chicks, and thought that they was puffins!

Now men was hard to find that spring or sailed we would have sooner,
For to our sorrow and despair, they shipped aboard our schooner.
On crossing Belle Isle Strait one night, the order from the skipper
Was, "Keep your canvas all drawn tight, and on your lee, the Dipper."
But 'fore the dawn there came a crash; from stem to stern a shiver;
And from our bunks we made a dash and heard a running river.
We found that Jimmie was at the helm and Stephen was the scunner.
That we still lived was good to feel when two such creatures run her.
Our waterline, a growler rived, and through the seams comes sievin'
The ocean roaring for the lives...of Jimmie Walsh and Stephen.

Our Guardian Angel never knew of such a busy season.
We kept our senses all alert and knew we had good reason.
Such constant strain near cracked me brain, so the sealing game I'm leaving.
And if I raise, give all the praise...to Jimmie Walsh and Stephen.

> —Sealers' song, c. 1870

> Jinker, *a Jonah, bearer of bad luck;*
> scunner, *lookout;* growler, *fragment of an iceberg;*
> rived, *punctured;* raise, *to quit.*

Sit ye down while I sings ye a ditty
Of the spring we was out in the Dan.
Maurice Crotty was one of our swilers–
A comical cure of a man!
It was his first spring at ice hunting,
Not a rope in the ship did he know.
Not even how to fold up a bunting,
And awkward to lace up a tow.
When the skipper sung out one fine morning,
"Come, Crotty, 'tis your trick at the wheel,"
Why he shook like a mouse on a skillet,
So timid and nervous did feel.

Once we passed near some steamers, lights blazing,
And Maurice he said unto me:
"Ain't that a fine sight, Mister Daley?
Sure, 'tis drugstores afloat on the sea.
...But do codfish have need of hop bitters?"
Says Maurice to me with a frown.
"Or is someone out here got the measles?
For 'tis strange to see drugstores lave town."

Well, we struck the whitecoats the next morning,
And over the side, every man,
With his gaff or his bat on his shoulder
Went copying over each pan.
But Maurice, a half mile behind us,
Was dancing all kinds of queer frills.
He was bowing and scraping on tiptoe
Like a man in a set of quadrilles.

We missed him all day, until evening.
I mind I had five young harps laced.
We was over four miles from our steamer,
A long road before us to face.
Coming home, 'bout a mile from the vessel,
We found Maurice stripped off for a bout,
And a big old dog hood, with his flippers,
Was stretching him out with each clout.
"I challenged him fair," said poor Maurice.
"For a fight he before me did stand.
But he took a mean, dirty advantage,
For he hit me...with rocks in his hand!"

–Sealers' song, c. 1900

Finding the whelping patch among those thousands of square miles of drifting, heaving ice was the vital element in the hunt. Sometimes the patch was never found and the ships came home empty. Sometimes it was found and could not be worked because of ice conditions. Sometimes it was found on a Sunday and, if the skipper of the ship was a practising Christian, that could be a special kind of disaster. Jacob Kelloway used to tell of one such occasion.

'Twere coming on duckish Saturday evening, and we'd been butting around in the ice for a week, and the ship was pretty well jammed, and not a sign of a patch of young seals had we seen when the scunner, up in the foremast barrel, lets out a whoop:

"Young fat to star-r-r-r-b'ard!"

All of a slam all hands was on deck and lining the rails. Skipper Tom was out on the wing of the bridge with his spyglass, pointing it all round the ice like an old brass cannon.

"How many and how far?" he bawls back to the barrelman.

"Scattered few 'bout a mile off nor'nor'east," comes the answer, "but I t'inks they's a gert patch a mile or two 'yond that."

All eyes was on the skipper. He paced up and down, chewing on his lip, as we waited to hear him give the order: "Over the side and make a rally, men!" But he never give it. 'Twas too dark and the sky was looking for weather. It must have near choked him to keep quiet, knowing the next day was Sunday, for Skipper Tom was a churchgoing man. There was nothing to be done but burn down where we was at till Monday morning and hope the patch wouldn't go abroad and none of them other ships would heave in sight.

That Sunday was the most tormenting day ever I spent. The white-coats was all 'round and singing so loud they near drowned out the hymn singing down below. Uncle Absolom Kelloway was our preacher, and he was so vexatious about them seals, he gave the Lord the rate word.

"Lard God," he hollers. "Blessin' on yer name! But what in hellfire's the use of puttin' we into such a pickle? We been right lang aboard o' this one and nary a pick o' fat to be had. Well, now Lard, we don't say 'tis all your fault, certainly, but we t'inks 'tis a wunnerful cold smack for ye to put we onto swiles on a Saturday night, and Sunday no more good to we than legs is to a fish! 'Tis an awful muckery ye got we into now, and we'm hopes you's all t'roo wit' trashin' we around like dat!"

Uncle Absolom laid it heavy enough, but the Lord never held it against us, for Monday morning come fine and warm and we killed and panned near three t'ousand seals that day.

The impression of an army setting out to do battle, given by the crew of one of the sealing steamers as they went on the ice, was more than skin-deep, for the sealers were organized almost on military lines. Before the ship reached the ice the men would have been divided into four watches, each under the command of a master watch who, in turn, divided his group into three sections. One of these he kept under his own control; the other two being commanded by his two junior officers – a bridgemaster and a scunner (more often called a deck robber).

As soon as the ship got into the whelping ice – into the fat – the four watches would muster on deck and await the captain's orders. As the vessel steamed along, he would call for a rally by one watch and the thirty to fifty men involved would scramble over the side, leaping wildly to get clear as the ship went on her way, sending the floes spinning and cracking in her wake.

Then the master watch would lead his crowd to the first good patch of young harp seals and there detach the scunner with his section. The bridgemaster and his group would be left at the next good patch and finally the master watch would pick a patch for himself and his men at "the end of the line," perhaps three or four miles from the point where they had gone on ice. By then the ship herself might have steamed clean out of sight, dropping the other watches along a course ten or fifteen miles long.

Each leader would always disperse his men in pairs so that if one plunged through the ice his chum could come to his rescue. Two or three particularly strong floes would be selected in the area being worked by each crowd and would be marked by numbered flags sporting the colours of the company that owned the ship.

So the men were scattered, often over a hundred square miles of ice, to kill and sculp the whitecoats wherever they could be found. A good man could sculp a hundred young seals in a day, but the real work lay in making the heavy fat-layered pelts into tows of four or five and then dragging them to the nearest flagged pan, which might be a mile away across broken, hummocked, shifting ice.

Ideally the ship would retrace her course in the evening to pick up the pans of fat and the sealers, but conditions at the ice were rarely ideal. It was all too common for pans of many hundreds of pelts to be left adrift for days – frequently to be lost forever when a storm came down. And it was no uncommon thing for the sealers to be left out overnight as well.

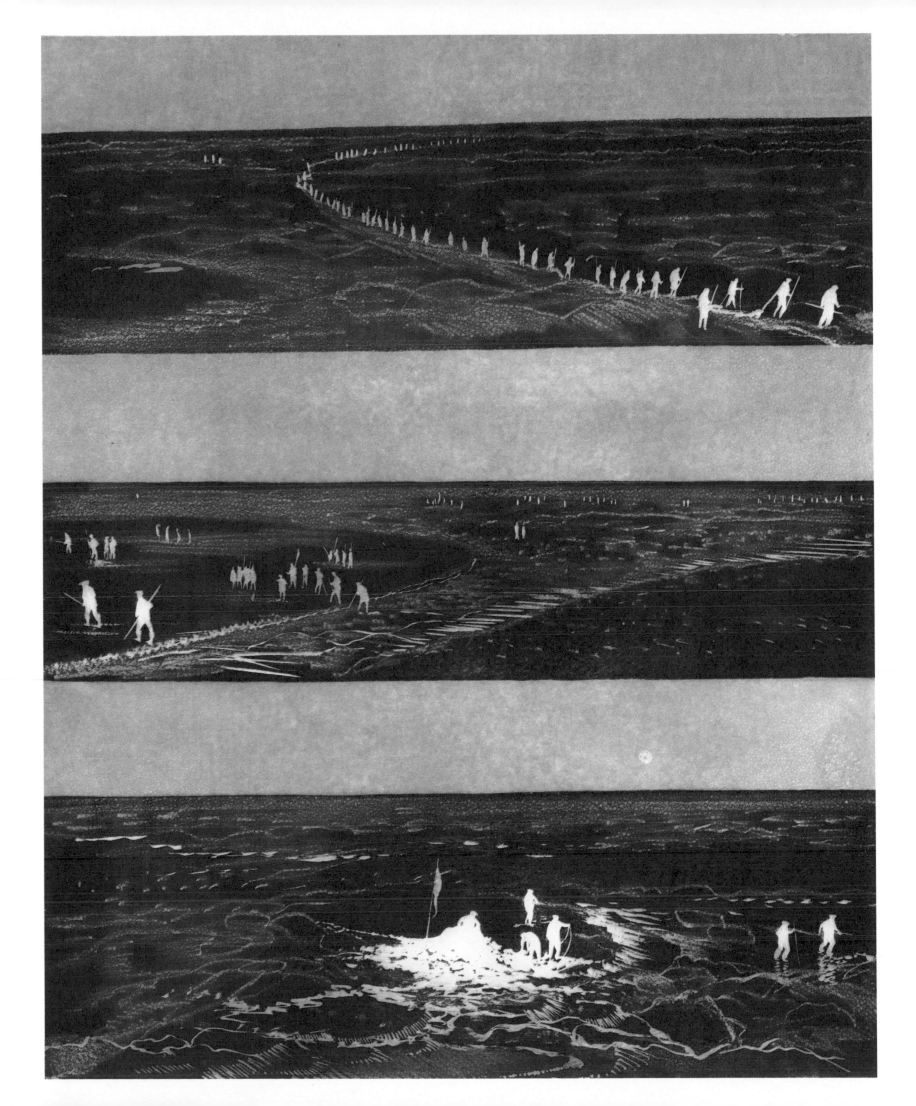

Written accounts of what it was like to be a sealer in those times are rare because most educated Newfoundlanders took care to have nothing to do with that dangerous aspect of the business. There was one remarkable exception: the Reverend Doctor M. Harvey, who was born into one of the Water Street families that had come to the top in the sealing game. At one time or another A. J. Harvey and Company owned a dozen sealing steamers and made a fortune out of them. Like most of the Water Street crowd, however, they gave a good deal more thought to the money than to the men, and it was a surprise for all hands when the Reverend Doctor joined one of the family ships in the spring of 1895 to see for himself what it was all about. The way the men and seals were treated upset him so much he published an account of it which nearly made him an outcast from his own family and from the rest of St. John's society.

Let us suppose the steamer has at last got sight of the seal patch. The whimpering of the young seals is heard, gladdening the hearts of the hunters...It is like the sobbing or mewling of an infant...No sooner is it heard than the vessel is laid-to, the men eagerly bound on the ice, and the work of destruction begun. A blow on the nose from a gaff shod with iron fractures the skull of the young seal. In a moment the knife is at work. The skin, with the fat adhering, is "sculped" from the carcass, which is left on the ice still quivering with life.

The work of slaughter goes on without cessation. The hunters scatter over the ice in all directions and often wander miles from their ships. The ice is soon stained with gore and dotted with the skinless carcasses of the slain. The deck becomes slippery with mingled blood and fat. Blood-gouts cover the hands and arms of the men. The shivering seals' low moans fill the air. What a scene, amidst these icy solitudes of the frozen ocean, with the bright sun lighting up the glittering pinnacles. The poor mother seals, now cubless, are seen popping their heads up in the small holes in the ice looking for their snow-white darlings and refusing to believe that the bloody carcasses on the ice are all that remains of their tender offspring. With a moan of distress they plunge into the sea as if anxious to escape from the ensanguined trail of the hunter.

As for the sealers, the perils of the ice field are neither few nor small and the hardships and exposure are such that only men of iron could endure. These men seem to have an absolute contempt for the terrors of floes and sea. They leap from pan to pan where it would seem a child could hardly be sustained, and think little of passing a night on ice far from the steamer. Should a fog or snowstorm set in, there is a terrible risk of losing their way and perishing miserably in these ice-deserts or of falling through the openings, which are covered with floating snow as it falls and freezes.

Sometimes the field-ice on which they work separates without a moment's warning into fragments, and they are floated off to perish by cold and hunger. The greatest danger of all is when a violent storm rages, breaking up the ice fields and driving before it the larger floes intermingled with fragments of arctic ice as hard as granite.

Woe to the vessel that is exposed to these ice giants! When the wild nor'easter rises, the great swell of the Atlantic, rolling in continuous ridges, heaves the pavement of ice into mighty folds. The whole mass contracts and expands and the broken fragments are dashed up on one another in hills of ice. Fragments rafter over each other in layers fifty feet thick. The thunderous crashes of the ice giants, combined with the roaring overhead of the gale and the blinding snowstorm, make up a scene of awe and terror. Then, at times, an iceberg takes part in the fray, sailing remorselessly forward, rending and tearing the ice field and scattering its fragments.

Such are the scenes amidst which the sealers gather in the "precious things of the deep."

–Adapted from Newfoundland in 1897
by Rev. Dr. M. Harvey

One of the few educated men I ever knew who went to the ice was a Wesleyville boy who grew up to be a teacher.

After my father and his older brother died in the Greenland disaster in 1898 – they froze to death with so many others – my mother made a vow that, come what might, none of us boys would ever go to the ice. Although hard times followed for our family, she not only kept her word but was very reluctant even to let my three brothers and me go fishing on the Labrador in the summers to make enough money for our schooling. "The sea took too many of our folk," she used to say. "It'll take no more of mine!"

She herself had been a teacher when she met my father, and she was determined I would be one too, for it was almost the only work a man could get in those days that did not take him on the sea. I won a scholarship finally and went to St. John's for teacher training. Then in 1928 I took the school at Newtown – that used to be called Pinchards Bight. That Christmas I got married and was in a fair way to being a happy man, but a few years later the hard times came again and things got very bad. There was no money to pay the teacher, and we had a small baby to keep. So I determined I would have to go sealing and hope to make a few dollars. That was in the spring of 1931.

For old times' sake, Captain William Kennedy, who was going navigator on the Viking with Captain Abraham Kean, Jr., son of the famous sealing captain of that name, procured a berth for me. Away I went to Gambo with the rest of the local men. It was a great thrill, indeed, for me, and I did not mind going in the least; but my poor old mother was heartbroken, being certain only bad would come of her broken vow.

As I recall there were about a hundred and fifty of us aboard the Viking, and we were mostly northern bay men. There were some jokes made about a man thirty years of age making his first trip to the ice, and I was known as Whitecoat, but it was good-natured, and I did not mind.

We put out on March 9th and were the last ship to sail for the front, being delayed by some American motion picture men who were to sail with us and take a picture of the hunt. Two days out from port we ran into a terrible storm in open water, the "blue drop," as the men called it. It was really a hurricane and seas were soon boarding the ship and sweeping her end for end. She laboured very heavily and began to take water so badly the engine-driven pumps could not hold it. A huge wave swept away our galley with all the cooking gear and the stove, and the cook barely escaped with his life. All of our boats were swept away as well, except one nest of dories, enough for perhaps a dozen men.

It was a bad lookout entirely, and I began to fear my poor old mother had been right, and I should have stayed ashore. However, with all hands at the pumps we somehow kept her afloat while Captain Kean worked her in to the lee of the land under Flowers Island, which was uninhabited by then and lay less than twenty miles from Newtown, which we could see in the distance but could not reach because of the ice. Here we rode out the storm for three days and made what repairs we could. I thought it would have been entirely likely the captain would give up the voyage because of the damage, but he was a Kean, and he had his father's reputation to maintain, so on Saturday, March 14th, we steamed out of the bay bound nor'west. We found the main ice near the Horse Islands and by evening were well into very heavy pack.

When I turned in that night I had a difficult time to go to sleep although I was done-in from working at the pumps. I could not get the thought of home and Newtown out of my head, but it was not my wife and child I thought about so much as my mother. At last I fell asleep, but I seemed to hear her as plain as I could hear the rasping of the ice against the hull. She was weeping and moaning the way she did for a long time, at night, after father's dreadful death.

And then, it seemed to me, I was wide awake and out on the ice in a terrible blizzard, searching for survivors from the Greenland. Suddenly two figures emerged from the drifting snow in front of me. I knew they were my father and my uncle. But they were not alive. They were dead men–frozen white–and stumbling toward me holding out their frozen arms...

I had no more sleep that night. I don't believe in ghosts and spirits, but, as the Lord is with me, it was a true warning from the other side.

The *Viking*, built at Arendal, Norway, in 1881, to the same design as the Scots whalers, was a 500-ton, ship-rigged wooden wall powered by an 86-horsepower engine. In 1904, when the Norwegians had no more use for her, she was bought by Bowring Brothers of St. John's and for the next twenty-seven springs went to the ice for that company in the sealing game. By the spring of 1931 she was a half-century old and showing her age. Decades of neglect and hard usage had, in the words of one of her last skippers, "fair taken the good right out of her." Nevertheless, she was still considered good enough to carry one hundred and fifty men into the most dangerous waters in the North Atlantic and into the violence of the pack ice.

In early March she put to sea under command of Captain Abraham Kean, Jr. Like so many of the sealing skippers, young Kean knew little navigation and was not a qualified master. So Bowrings had been forced, by law, to ship a certified master as well. He was Captain William Kennedy, age twenty-nine, who had just been accepted as a seagoing officer by one of the large British freighter lines. Since he was not to take over his new job until summer and because times were hard, he was glad to earn a few dollars shipping aboard the *Viking* – although the orders of the owners, that he was not to interfere with the operation of the ship, did not please him. He was, in fact, little more than a passenger aboard.

In addition to her sealers, the *Viking* carried an unusual extra complement, an American film crew led by Varick Frissell, who were making a romantic film about sealing to be called *Northern Knight*. They were all young men and, in truth, the *Viking* was a young man's ship that spring, for the great majority of her officers and men were in their twenties, driven to the ice by the urgent financial need of those depression years.

Having barely weathered a hurricane on her way to the front, the *Viking* finally took the ice late on Saturday, March 14th. The pack was exceptionally heavy and after a few hours Captain Kean decided to burn down for the night in a polynia, or open lake, among the floes. He went early to his cabin, leaving his officers and the film-makers to sit a while, drink tea, and yarn in the tiny saloon where the bogey stove glowed red-hot as protection against the bitter night. Under the saloon table slept a massive black Newfoundland dog named Cabot, belonging to Varick Frissell. The dog kept whining uneasily until one of the Americans, Henry Sargent, bent down and fondled its head. Frissell was busy printing large letters on a piece of cardboard. Clayton King, the *Viking*'s twenty-two-year-old Marconi operator, peered over his shoulder and read the words aloud: "Notice! DANGER! POWD . . . er." The final two letters had not yet been added, but Clayton voiced them anyway.

The Newfoundlanders in the saloon – with the exception of Kennedy – were amused. What was the danger in powder? Every ship going to the ice carried as much as a ton of blasting powder and dynamite, together with dozens of cases of rifle ammunition for the adult seal hunt. When a ship got jammed, the men freed her with explosives which they treated as casually as they treated most other things aboard those ships.

The *Viking*'s magazine was a small room just off the saloon. It was too small for its job, so several cases of powder and ammunition had been stored across the narrow hall in a tiny, doorless cubicle that also held the vessel's only toilet. It was perfectly normal for a sealer to be seated on the throne smoking his pipe or knocking the glowing dottle out against one of the cans of blasting powder. This spectacle had appalled the Americans and, after discussing it with Captain Kennedy, Frissell had decided to put up a warning sign.

The sign was never completed. The ship suddenly lurched violently to starboard, heeling over so sharply that the bogey fell on its side, spilling burning coals all over the floor and down the alleyway. The men slid off their benches into a heap against a transverse bulkhead. While they were sorting themselves out, Captain Kean burst from his cabin and, only half-dressed, stumbled out on the bridge as the ship gradually righted herself.

He saw at once what had happened. The wind had changed; the "ice claw" anchor holding the ship to the edge of the floe had torn loose and the *Viking* had gone charging across the polynia to bring up hard against the further edge. Captain Kean was just about to call the bo's'n to put another ice claw out and make fast when the whole stern of the ship buckled beneath his feet. He was flung far out over the ice in the red glare of a tremendous explosion. The *Viking*'s magazine had gone up with a colossal roar . . . in a pillar of flame!

Of the dozen men in the saloon, only three survived. One of them was Clayton King who wrote a pamphlet about his experiences. This excerpt begins after he had crawled to the stern of the burning *Viking.*

Looking around me I saw nothing but wreckage. The ship had been blown almost to the water's edge...the ice was aglow from the flames. Cries for help were everywhere. On one ice pan I saw a man in a pool of blood–a deep gash in his head.

"Who are you?" I cried.

"Kennedy. Come and help me."

"Can't make it. My legs are all smashed up."

Another explosion shattered the hull and a body came hurtling out of the wreckage to land on an ice pan close to the ship. The man's head split open to his neck. With a few convulsive movements his body slid off the pan into the sea.

I felt the cords on my neck drawing taut with the heat. Get clear, I must. I either fell or threw myself and landed in the water. Henry Sargent came to my rescue and pulled me out. After heroic work he was able to move Kennedy and myself from danger. As the fire reached deeper into the hull there were more explosions. Black clouds of smoke belched from her deck. Figures, grotesque in the light of the flames, were falling over the side...

We three drifted away from the wreck...Sargent got me and Kennedy on a piece of wreckage from the Viking's stern. This, supported by an ice pan, was the safest place for a while at least. As the night wore on the wind came howling out of the north. The hours went by. The dawn came and the sun shone brightly with a blue-white glare. We were drifting fast. For twenty-two miles from where the Viking went down we drifted in the ice of the desolate Atlantic.

Monday I was only conscious intermittently. Tuesday I heard Sargent raving: "God! What am I going to do? Kennedy is dying and King is dead!" Later I heard Kennedy breathing very heavily and guessed he had pneumonia.

In my next conscious period I heard Sargent shouting: "Hurrah! Hurrah! It's a steamer...I can see her hull!"

As a rescue boat from the S.S. Sagona reached the ice pan I heard one of the crew exclaim: "Look at King's legs!" I looked at them myself. My right one was twisted up alongside my body, the bone exposed and the frost shining through the lacerated flesh. I drifted off into a coma and when I woke again someone patted me on the shoulder, saying: "King, you are all right now."

–Adapted from The Viking's Last Cruise
by Clayton L. King

King was all right – if losing both legs to the hip from gangrene is "all right," but at least he survived. Kennedy did not, nor did twenty-eight others of the *Viking*'s crew. The survival of many of the rest was survival only, for a great number suffered crippling injuries from which they never recovered. The majority managed to make their way over the ice to the isolated Horse Islands, where the local Marconi operator, Otis Bartlett, became a Newfoundland hero by reporting their terrible plight to the outer world and by directing a rescue fleet of sealing ships and other vessels to the disaster area. The film-maker, Varick Frissell, and Cabot, the big black dog that had whined uneasily under the saloon table, were among those who were never seen again.

The wooden walls did not always die by accident – sometimes they were murdered.

The *Diana* began life in 1869 as the whaler *Hector*. A whaling ship's life in the arctic seas was hard enough, but in 1871 her Scots owners decided to squeeze even more work out of her by sending her to the Newfoundland seal fishery each spring and then her life grew harder still. In February of each year thereafter she fought her way across the winter North Atlantic to St. John's, took on a crowd of sealers and headed out to the whelping ice where she butted and pounded about among the floes, often until early May. Returning to St. John's she would discharge seals and sealers and then shape her course northward to spend an icebound summer cruising for bowheads in Davis Strait and Baffin Bay. When the autumnal gales began she would go labouring homeward to Dundee again, a weary ship, worn with the travail in the ice. This was her life until 1892, but at least her Scots owners gave her some kindness in midwinter, when she was laid up, and kept her in good condition.

Things changed for her when she was bought by a St. John's firm in '92, renamed *Diana*, and given over completely to the sealing game. During each of the remaining years of her life she seldom came alive except for the two or three months when she went sealing. For the rest, she mostly lay,

dirty, neglected, dying by degrees, moored with her sister wooden walls at the south side of St. John's harbour.

In the spring of 1922 she was fifty-three years old and for years past had received only the most cursory attention and minimal repairs. Her ancient engine was little more than a pile of junk. Her masts and spars were brittle and cracked with age; her sails were not much better than patched dusters. Below the waterline, rot and sea worms had finally begun to win their victory over her massive timbers and planking. She leaked at almost every seam; her too-few lifeboats were baskets that would have filled instantly had they ever been lowered. Everyone knew she was unfit to go to sea, and this included her owners as well as the one hundred and sixty-seven men who were to sail in her.

She war no better nor a death trap, and we'm all knowed it, sure. But what was we to do? Was no other berths for we in ary other ship. 'Twas the devil's choice, bye. Five or six older chaps left her, certainly, and went ashore. 'Twas all right for they, but we knowed as any man refused to sail would never get another berth on ary vessel out of St. John's. The owners would see to that. So the most of we stayed aboard she for the voyage.

She sailed on March 10th under command of a hardcase skipper of whom it was said that he valued a good fat seal over any sealer who had ever lived. Perhaps that was a lie, but it was true enough that he did not seem to value human life very highly, and it was his boast that he would sail a log to the front if there was no other command available to him.

It was a bad spring for ice, with the floes close-packed and spiked with innumerable bergs and growlers. Heavy easterly gales kept the field compacted, jamming most of the vessels of the sealing fleet but sending the big bergs plunging through the raftered ice as if it had no more substance than tissue paper. Twice *Diana* found herself jammed and in the path of one of these blind behemoths, and once a cliff of ice ripped through the pack so close alongside that it snagged the end of her main yard and splintered it to bits.

The ice was bad, the weather ferocious – but the sealing was good. Most of the ships were in the main patch and, because of the tight ice, the men could hunt far and wide among the whitecoats. By March 21st the *Diana's* hard-driven, half-starved, and increasingly sullen crew had stowed away something between 14,000 and 19,000 pelts (the true number was never known), and the men were praying for the ice pressure to ease so that the leaking, creaking old hulk could make her cut for home.

The pressure did not ease. Instead, it grew worse. The floes began to rafter into ridges thirty and forty feet high that came hard against the sides of the old wooden wall. She groaned, and her timbers writhed under the mounting pressure. She began to open up until her pumps could hardly cope with the inflow.

Now even her hardcase skipper grew apprehensive that the old ship would not survive and so he secretly arranged by coded wireless with a sister ship owned by the same firm to have her take on as much as she could carry of *Diana's* cargo of prime young fat. Then he ordered his crew to begin putting the sculps back on ice and to pan them at a safe distance from the ship. At the same time he assured them the vessel was in no danger.

The men were not stupid. They were convinced that when the ice slackened *Diana* would go down, leaving the sister ship to pick up the fat and to claim it as salvage. That way the owners would suffer no loss, but the sealers of the *Diana* stood to lose the handful of dollars their unimaginably hard labours had earned for them.

So there was a "manus" – a mutiny. The men refused to unload a single pelt unless the captain guaranteed them their share when the fat reached St. John's. However, the captain would promise nothing. He and his officers armed themselves and held the bridge.

The impasse lasted for two days while the sister ship, which had been unlucky in the hunt and only had a few thousand sculps of her own, lay waiting like a jackal in heavy ice several miles away. She kept her distance, and the *Diana's* crew believed this was deliberate – that she would not rescue them until they had put their seals on ice. On the morning of the third day of the manus they made up their minds to break the deadlock their own way – or at least some among them did.

Shortly after dawn the fearful cry of "FIRE!" rang out. There was no more than enough time for all hands to gain the ice before the old vessel, her every plank and timber soaked through and through with oil and her holds filled with seal fat, became a roaring pyre. She burned so fiercely that men on the *Terra Nova*, fifteen miles away, were awed by the pillar of smoke that towered into a white and cloudless sky.

She burned so fast and furiously that panic gripped her people and they fled, a streaming mob, across the ice for the shelter of the distant sister ship.

The fire was so terrible hot we was feared the ice would melt under we. That was foolishness, of course, but 'twas such an awful sight to see her burn, with all that fat aboard.

How did it happen then? They's none as ever would say for sure, but this I knows. Yiss, by the Powers, we was all agreed that if we was to lose our voyage, the merchants in St. John's would never take a nickle profit out of it! Nor did they. No, they couldn't even sell she to the insurance companies, for none of they was daft enough to place a dollar on the old Diana.

So the *Diana* died at the hands of her own men. But perhaps murder is too hard a term for what they did, for it was a true Viking funeral they gave her at the end of her long years.

Disasters at the ice were so commonplace that most of them were soon put out of mind – except by those who survived or by the families of those who did *not* survive. Those who went to the ice lived with the near certainty that they would be involved in a disaster sooner or later and, in some almost masochistic way, they seemed to embrace the prospect. " 'Twas as if a man never felt hisself to be a proper swiler 'less he'd been on talking terms with death a time or two."

However, if the sealers had come to a fatalistic acceptance of danger, disfigurement, and death among the northern floes, those who exposed them to it – the owners of the sealing industry, who were the autocracy of Newfoundland – were equally unconcerned. St. John's *was* Newfoundland to them, while we outport people dwelt somewhere in limbo. The writers of the island's history were *of* St. John's; and so, during the nearly one hundred years that the seal fishery was conducted under sail from the outport settlements, most of the men and ships that were lost were seldom even mentioned in the records. They lived in limbo, they died in limbo and were conveniently forgotten. It was not quite the same with the steam fleet and their crews, for these ships were owned in St. John's, sailed from there and, when they failed to return, could not be entirely ignored. Some records of the steamer losses, even if these only consist of a few words in an old St. John's paper, still exist.

During the thirty years between 1870 and 1900 the sealing steamers *Bloodhound* (first), *Wolf* (first) and *Wolf* (second), *Retriever, Osprey, Ariel, Tigress, Hawk, Mic Mac, Tiger, Resolute, Winsor Lake,* and *Mastiff* were all crushed and sunk in the grinding pack. The *Lion* disappeared without a trace, with her entire crew, while heading for the ice. The year before the *Tigress* was crushed, her decrepit boiler exploded and killed twenty-one men. In 1889 the *Walrus* lost twenty-five men who went adrift in the pack and were never found. Five years later eight more men were killed and the *Walrus* was nearly sunk by a powder explosion.

Because the sealing industry was by this time concentrated in St. John's, whose merchants still sent a number of sailing ships to the ice, some of the sailing fleet did manage to find their way into the written history of the seal fishery. They included the *Huntsman,* lost with forty-five men; *Dundonald,* thirty-three men lost; *Village Belle,* eighteen drowned; *Deerhound,* forty-four lost; *Emerald,* thirty-eight lost; *Northland,* thirty lost.

These were a few of the sealing disasters during these three decades, but the near-disasters were even more numerous. One March day in 1890 the *Terra Nova, Eagle,* and two other steamers had their entire crews, totalling more than five hundred men, on ice in dubious weather when a blizzard swept over the floes. In their ferocious competition with each other the steamer captains had spread their men for twenty or thirty miles over the pack and, with the onset of the storm, had no chance of finding them again until the storm ended. It did not abate for three days and nights and, but for a miracle, most of the sealers would have perished.

The miracle was the presence on the scene of the little *Kite,* underpowered, ancient, and unable to dash off through the pack scattering her men broadcast as her bigger rivals had done. She lay jammed in the middle of the main patch. Her own men were out, so the *Kite* kept her whistle blowing all through the balance of that day and far into the night to guide them back to safety. Fortunately she had a disproportionately loud voice and the abandoned sealers from the other ships also homed on it, so that dawn found the *Kite* playing host to her own one hundred and fifty-six men plus five hundred and forty freezing and starving strangers! Unable to take them all aboard, the *Kite*'s master provided coal and wood for fires on the ice, canvas for rough shelters, and a supply of tea and hardtack until the storm ended and the men could be picked up by their own ships.

That was a desperately near thing, but it had no perceptible effect on the behaviour of the ships' owners. The Newfoundland government, which the merchants effectively controlled, continued to refuse to enact any significant legislation to prevent further additions to the long list of disasters, on the grounds that any such laws would interfere with the owners' God-given right to make the greatest possible profit from the seal fishery. As one official publicly stated: "The financial stability of our island home depends to a large degree upon a flourishing and successful seal fishery. It is our bounden duty, therefore, to ensure that nothing interferes with the gathering of the great harvest of the ice fields, whose failure must inevitably work fearful hardship upon the lives of all our people."

He was, of course, speaking of economic hardship. The other kind could be disregarded or, when it was brought to public notice, could be hailed as evidence of our sealers' patriotic qualities.

Occasionally, after a particularly horrendous disaster, the townspeople of St. John's would acknowledge the tragedy in the local newspapers, pointing out that the dead were safe in heaven where they were much better off than ever they had been while still alive.

"These fine fellows died at duty's call...They are in God's keeping and there they will rest with the Merciful Father who does not permit even a sparrow to fall unnoticed, and who was with them in their darkest hour."

So quoth the mayor of St. John's, himself a prosperous merchant, after a particularly ghastly disaster at the ice.

The newspapers would also sometimes publish an inch or two of memorial tribute to the dead, praising the hardihood and courage of the sealers who were prepared to "die gallantly, in duty's traces." The following appeared in a St. John's paper after the S.S. *Newfoundland* disaster:

INDUSTRIAL SOLDIERS GO DOWN IN FIGHT

We ask: why did you, knowing the hazardous occupation of sealing, face its perils and dangers? The answer is one that inspires our Faith in Man! It was Duty's Call, and you obeyed. Were a monument to be erected to your memory, the epitaph could be inscribed: Sacred to those brave and hardy soldiers of the Industrial Army who struggled, suffered and died on the Frozen Battlefield for their Captains of Industry, and their loved ones at home. R.I.P.

Memorial poems were also written and published by the English-educated offspring of St. John's merchants. Presumably these were intended to bring comfort to the widows and children of our dead, although most outport people never saw a paper and couldn't have read one anyway.

Away far out on the Northern Floe
Labour the men of our Isle,
And they fight the grim Boreal blasts
With their cheerful native smile.

And when the Storm King reigns supreme,
They honour their native land,
And give their lives on the stormy floe,
Those heroes in heart and hand....

Perhaps these effusions were not really meant for the sealers or their families at all. Perhaps they were meant, instead, to ease the conscience of the St. John's elite who were responsible for the disasters. They may have served this purpose, but certainly they did nothing to prevent further tragedies from taking place. Death on the ice for the outport men was something the owners and rulers of our Island could easily take for granted even when, in the spring of 1898, just eight years after the near-loss of over five hundred men at the ice fields, there occurred an event that ought to have shaken their placid conviction that human sacrifice was quite in order so long as commerce prospered.

Sad comes the news across the sea, across the troubling main,
To fill the hearts of those they loved with sorrow and with pain.
'Tis less than three short weeks ago they left their native shore,
And many, alas, they have never returned to see their friends no more.

The Greenland sailed the tenth of March. Her crew in spirits gay
Stood brisk upon the barricade as she steamed out that day.
They were a crowd of fine young men who left in spirits light,
Not thinking that they would pass off, that fearful cold March night.
They struck the seals St. Patrick's Day, and then the work began,
With thirteen thousand pelts aboard, seven thousand more did pan.
Onto the thirty-first of March, four watches went that day,
A blinding snowstorm soon come on, and they got cast away.
There's two young Quidi Vidi boys, there's Charlie and Court Down;
There's William Collins from Torbay, and two from St. John's town.
The others from the northern bays, and six from Harbour Grace,
Who on that wild and stormy night, a fearful death did face....

–Sealers' song, c. 1898

94

It was the great dream of every Newfoundland boy to make a voyage to the ice, and the youngsters of St. John's — "carner byes," we used to call them contemptuously — were not immune. Few of them ever got berths because they weren't really fit for the life, but I knew of one exception — a young man apprenticed as a pharmacist's assistant who got the chance to ship aboard the S.S. *Greenland* in the spring of 1898.

The law called for a doctor to sail on every sealing ship, but of course the owners would not hire a real doctor even if one could be found who would have gone. Instead, any man who could read the label on a pill bottle or who claimed to be a hand at doctoring would fill the bill. Compared to most, I was pretty well trained and Captain Arch Davis, commanding the Greenland, was right content when I agreed to sign on with him.

The fleet sailed from St. John's on March 10, 1898, and the little Greenland was jammed up with one hundred and fifty-four sealers, plus the officers and engine-room crowd that amounted to fifteen more. It was a bad year for ice. The heaviest kind of old arctic pack was pushed south right into the land. Only a few days out, and before ever a ship had got into the seals, the Mastiff got nipped so bad she had to be abandoned and went down.

It was a bad start, certainly, but none of the other ships turned back. There was no getting deep into the fields, so the fleet hung on the eastern edge. On March 16th there come a westerly gale that opened the ice up a bit, and all the ships cut westward into it, following the leads when they could. Next day the Neptune, in the van, struck into the young seals and by nightfall every vessel was into the patch and all hands was on ice.

All the next week the men were away from the ship from dawn until dark and there was little enough for the "doctor" to do. Most of the sealers, specially the northern bay men, thought it a weakness to admit they was ever sick or hurt. Just the same, a number got "seal finger" and had to come to me. That was some kind of infection they'd get when they nicked a finger with their bloodstained old sculping knives. We treated it with raw carbolic acid poured on after it had been lanced, but often enough that did no good. Then the finger would have to be cut off or the infection would spread and kill the man. One of our master watches had lost four fingers that way, two from each hand. I had to cut off the forefinger of a man myself, without anything to ease his pain except a drink of rum.

Despite bad weather, the sealing was good and all ships were making a good showing. By March 30th we had about thirteen thousand pelts aboard and the men had panned another six or seven thousand. Panning seal sculps was done to save time so the sealers from one ship could kill all the seals in reach and not let other crews get them first. A ship might string her men out over twenty miles, all busy panning and moving on again. But when she came to pick up those pans she might not find the half of them.

The morning of March 31st the ice got loose and the weather mild, and some of our men looked for a storm. Just the same, all four watches was sent out. There was only scattered seals left by then so the men had to go far afield; some of them six or seven miles from the ship and mostly to westward where the ice was tighter.

Early evening, about three o'clock it was, the wind began to blow a hurricane with driving snow, and the temperature dropped right out – well below freezing. The gale was so heavy it caught the Greenland broadside where she lay in an open lead and heeled her over so all the loose pelts on deck slid into the lee scuppers and she nearly went right on over! For a time we were in a desperate state because we couldn't get her righted with the few hands left on board, and the stokers couldn't stand up to fire the boilers and keep steam on her.

Luckily one of the watches was close enough to the ship when the gale struck to get back aboard. All hands went at it then, shifting ballast and trimming coal and, after dark it was, the ship was upright and we had steam on the engine and the pumps. By then it was too late to try and pick up the rest of our men, for the wind was a living gale and thick of snow besides.

When dawn came the Greenland was jammed in heavy ice that was driving seaward. Westward of us, and between us and the men, a lake had opened near half a mile across. The barrelman could catch glimpses of our fellows on the other side of the lake, huddled up in black patches on the ice, but the ship could not get to them, nor them to us. Captain Davis was pretty near frantic, for he thought to lose them all. The cold was enough to kill a man outright. In the afternoon there come a lull and the captain sent every able-bodied man to haul our boats to the near edge of the lake and try to go for the stranded sealers. The fellows with those boats took some awful risks but they ended up saving a good many men. Most of the fellows in one watch that was off more to the northward contrived to get around the lake and back to the ship. By nightfall we had a hundred men aboard but fifty or more was still adrift. By then the temperature was below zero and we never thought to see any of them live through the night.

Next day the storm let up. The Greenland worked clear of the jam and went after the missing men. There was only a few of them alive, and they was in terrible bad shape. We picked up twenty bodies and five men so far gone they died aboard ship. The rest of the forty-eight men as was lost that day was never seen again by mortal eye.

The voyage home was the most desperate time of my life. I had to set-to and try to save the lives and limbs of dozens of men frost-burned almost to death. It was a nightmare to me but must have been all of that again for the sick men crowded into the cold 'tween deck space.

To make all worse, we met another gale as we neared land and the old engine give out and the Greenland blew onto the rocks near Bay de Verde and was near a total loss with all aboard. A lucky shift of the wind took us off before she broke up, and we somehow limped into St. John's with a cargo of dead seals under hatches and a cargo of dead men roped in a heap on the foredeck.

I never went sealing again. Nor ever wanted to.

There was times during that forty-eight hours when things wasn't too bad...like the feeling that rose in me when the sound of the storm was drowned out by the voices of the men raised in the hymn "Oh God, Our Help in Ages Past." Then there was other times, times when friends and shipmates struggled up to you and asked you into their house for a cup of tea! Then they would just vanish into the storm again before you could even stop them.

On the second day of the storm all of us were seeing things. A group of fifteen, myself included, thought we saw our ship in the ice on the horizon. We set out from the solid ice over the slob ice toward her. We scrambled all day on our hands and knees and in our wake was a trail of blood from our bleeding hands and knees. I realized after a while it was all a dream. There was no ship. I told the men to follow me back to the main ice and four of them did, but the other ten perished there among the slob.

We found a few seals on the main ice and killed them and used their skins for shelter, drank their blood and ate their meat. The next day we really did sight the ship and she finally came up to us...only four left out of the fifteen.

–John Melendy, S.S. Greenland *survivor*

If anything was going to change the attitude of the Water Street crowd toward the seal hunt and the sealers, it should have been the appalling homecoming of the battered *Greenland* with her gruesome deck cargo in full and horrifying view. But Water Street was proof even against such a shocking display as this. There were some pious professions of distress in the newspapers and some of the usual heroic versifying. A subscription was taken up on behalf of the wives and children of the dead men, and each bereaved family got about ten dollars. However, this was a *public* subscription and not compensation paid by the owners of the *Greenland*. They paid nothing although the bodies of our northern bay men were shipped home at the expense of the owners – in makeshift crates made from scraps of condemned lumber, and the men still clad in the tattered clothes in which they had died. Some of these "coffins" fell apart during the train journey to Gambo and it was said that several corpses had to be hauled out of the boxcars with ropes because they were so badly decayed.

There was no investigation into the disaster and, far from improving, the conditions endured by the men grew worse. This was not the time for reform of the seal fishery – competition for the remaining seals was growing fiercer as the herds dwindled in size. The merchants reasoned that if the high level of profits was to be maintained they would have to reduce operating costs. Sealers were one of those costs and sealing ships were another. Since there was an oversupply of both, it made good commercial sense to treat them as expendable items.

To some extent the sealers could be expected to look after themselves, since they were usually only at the ice for six or eight weeks and had the rest of the year to recover from that ordeal. This was not true of the ships. With the arrival on the scene of the first steel ice-breaking sealers, in 1906, the wooden walls became even more neglected. Most of them had become so unseaworthy that no insurance company would cover them and, even by the lax standards prevailing in St. John's, they ought to have been condemned out of hand. But it was the policy of the owners to let the ice "condemn" them.

In the five years between 1907 and 1912 the following wooden walls were lost in the ice: *Leopard* and *Greenland* in 1907 (the *Greenland* survived the death of so many of her men by just nine years); *Panther, Grand Lake,* and *Walrus* in 1908; *Vanguard* and *Virginia Lake* in 1909; *Iceland* in 1910; *Harlaw* in 1911; and *Labrador* in 1912. Some of these were crushed when their captains, increasingly desperate to make a good showing for the owners, put their ships into fatal jeopardy. More were lost when they broke down, blew up, or simply opened up and sank as the inevitable result of decades of neglect. As competition for the remaining seals continued to increase, some captains become so careless about the way they put men on ice that it became almost the accepted thing for parties of fifty or more men to find themselves spending a night on the floes when their ship was too busy elsewhere to come and pick them up.

We never knowed they was adrift until night fell. By then
there was a living starm from southerly with blinding snow.
All night the bo's'n kept the whistle moaning through the muck.
Their master watch burned flares. Two days blew by,
the wind veered northerly—a bitter blast. But all the same
we thought to try our luck at finding them. Bad ice
was all about. Black water smoking in the cruel frost.
The ship tight jammed; we walked three mile before the light
began to fail; by then she'd almost vanished in the drift.
'Twas time to give it up. John climbed a pinnacle
for one last look...and spied the figure of a man
lurching amongst the clumpers in the distant east.
We fired guns, waved flags, and bawled at him to come.
He heard. Stopped for a moment, turned from side to side
like a blind child.

And then...began to run
away from we! Run? *More like a bird he was, the way he flew*
over the heaving pack; dodging from sight like a black fox
behind each raftered floe; skipping across the slob
like he had wings, but never knew which way he had to go.

...We done our best. Chased after till our lungs
was choked, but lost him in the veil of water smoke.

We never saw the hide nor hair of him again. No more his chums.
He must have been the last one left alive. Poor lad!
Went mental in the head. I think he never knew
but what we was the dead...come back to claim him too.

The hypnotic world of ice had strange effects upon many of the sealers and there were few of them who, at one time or another, did not see strange objects and images. Some of the visions may have been due to the agonizing ice blindness resulting from the concentrated glare of sunlight on the glittering plains; but other things they saw were not so easily explained, as with this tale that Jacob Mullet used to tell.

Fifty-one springs to the ice and forty-three a master watch...they's not much I hasn't seen out there. Some says the ice's a lonely place, but I never found it so. Lots of life out on the ice. They's the swiles, of course, and what a sight it be when the old 'uns haul out for their enj'yin' time after the whitecoats dips—takes to the water. I been in the barrel on a fine sunny day and they was nothing to be seen far as the eye could go, only swiles lying about on the pans as thick as pepper, sunning theirselves. T'ousands and t'ousands; and more t'ousands leaping and breaching in the leads and lakes....And one time I was on ice and we come on a white bear, big as a house he was, and he took we for swiles and come for we hell-a-humping till he was no more'n a chain off, and we fellows with nothing but our gaffs. It looked like a tight squeeze, but old Uncle Benjamin Sturges, belonged to Cape Freels, he takes a jump for the bear and gives a shout: "Git out of it now, you big white buggar! Git out, damn ye, or I'll bite the black nose off your h'ugly face!" And would ye believe it, byes? That bear he turned and hauled his wind and we never see him after!...Aye and the little white foxes would be out there, t'ousands of miles from the arctic where they come from; and ice birds; and big black ravens come off from land to look for the carcasses. The sharks liked swile carcasses some good too. I've stood on a pan and gaffed a dozen and hauled 'em out. One time we used to take their livers and put 'em in a puncheon and sell 'em when we got back to St. John's.

Yiss, me sons, I seen it all...but they's some things I didn't care about. I remembers the spring of 1911 when I went master watch on the Newfoundland. Young Wes Kean, son of old Captain Abe, was master of her and 'twas his first command. 'Twas a good spring...moderate weather and the whitecoats thick as flies on the flake in August. We done very good.

One morning, near the end of March, Skipper Wes put me and my watch of forty men out in a scattered patch of "rusty-coats"—young swiles getting their dark hair and near ready to dip. Wes steamed away to see could he find more swiles for the rest of the crowd and the ship was near out of sight when it come on to starm, right sudden. I got my crowd together in a hurry and I says: "Well, lads, us'd best give this up and make for the ship. Skipper'l never find we now, but we might find he."

I thought he might stay where he was to. I had a good compass and I knowed I could lay a cut handy enough to hear the whistle for a guide.

'Twas no Sunday courting stroll we had that day. The ice was open and the leads full of slob and half the men got ducked before we come to a great big lead. There was no crossing she at all. So then there was nothing to be done but find a pan of thick old ice and put up for the night. After dark the wind hauled nor'ard and it got colder than a merchant's heart.

We was all near froze and pretty well bate-out by then. A good many of the men lay down to take a rest in the shelter of a line of clumpers. I lit some flares and sot meself down on a piece of ice and I supposes I dozed off, for the next thing I knowed I was looking up the path from the landwash to my own house. 'Twas clear as the real thing. But the old Union Jack I always used to fly alongside was hauled down to half-mast. They was a big crowd gathered round—people I knowed as well as I knows meself—and they was all waiting for something. Then the front door, as we never uses, swings open and out comes a coffin with me woman and me youngsters walking behind it, all crying and carrying on. I knowed right away 'twas my own coffin.

Then the quarest thing ever come over I. Up I jumps from that piece of ice, all standing. I'd been near perished when I sot down, but now I felt fit as a young fellow going off to a dance...and that's what I had in mind...to go to a dance!

'Twas only a minute until I had the whole crowd on their feet. Them as couldn't or wouldn't budge, I kicked them till they did.

"Git up and come to the dance!" I shouted. "Or, be Jasus, I'll kill ye if ye don't!"

Some told me afterwards they was certain I'd gone off cat-crazy, but they was feared to go agin me. The truth on it was, me mind was clear as it is today. But 'twas like some stranger had stepped into me skin and "Dance!" says he. And dance we did till the blood was moving again and there was no more chance we'd freeze to death.

We was still at it, bawling out the old songs and jigging like a proper crowd of loonies, when out of the dark of the starm comes the blare of a steamer's siren. In a minute the old Newfoundland hove in sight, all lights lit and shining, and flares lining her barricade till she looked like she was all afire. When we was aboard again they told us they'd have missed us sure, only they heard the hullabaloo we was making from down-wind and found us so.

'Twas a quare thing, certainly; for what would make a man dance at his own funeral? And that was just what I done.

By 1900 the seal fishery was in the hands of only a few St. John's merchants, of whom the most famous – or infamous, depending on your point of view – were A. J. Harvey and Company, Bowring Brothers Ltd., Job Brothers and Company, and Baine, Johnson and Company. These four set the rules of the game, decided the price of fat, and took the lion's share of the profits; but with the continuing decline in the seal herds, each was constantly seeking a means of gaining an advantage over its rivals.

In 1906 Harveys jumped into the lead by building a steel ship for the sealing. The S.S. *Adventure* was a wonder for her time: an 800-tonner with a 200-horsepower engine, specially designed for the ice to a new and daring plan. Her forefoot was cut away so that, instead of trying to split, or butt the pans aside, she could ride right up onto them, breaking and separating them with her weight and her momentum.

At first the old sealing hands, including the directors of the rival companies, thought Harveys had gone mad. "A steel ship like that," they scoffed, " will be crushed in the ice like a sardine can. There's no give to her plates. It'd be suicide, sure, to go to the pack in her!"

This belief was so widespread that Harveys had a job to get a crew for the *Adventure* and she was forced to sail with less than half the men she could have carried. But once in the ice she soon proved herself. She was twice as handy and twice as fast as any of the old wooden walls. She could get along through ice where none of them could follow, and she made a bumper voyage. When she sailed back through the Notch into St. John's harbour, there were some glum faces at Bowrings and Jobs, for she had made it clear that the days of the wooden walls were now numbered.

By 1909 Harveys, well satisfied, had built two more steel steamers, the *Bonaventure* and the *Bellaventure* – 500-tonners with 300-horsepower engines. Striving to catch up, Bowrings built the 2,000-ton, 450-horsepower *Florizel*, and Jobs commissioned the *Beothic*, of the same class as the *Belle* and the *Bon*. In 1912 Jobs added the 1,000-ton *Nascopie*, but Bowrings topped all competition with the 2,100-ton, 600-horsepower *Stephano*. All of these ships were intended to serve as sealers in the spring but as passenger vessels or freighters for the balance of the year.

The coming of the steel fleet brought competition for the remaining seals to a new and frantic pitch. Risks were taken with men and ships that startled sealers who had been going to the ice for half a century. This was especially true with the old wooden walls who, though they were now badly outclassed, still outnumbered the steel steamers. What had been foolhardy daring by captains in the past now became suicidal daring as the skippers of the wooden walls tried desperately to make good showings. By 1914 the competition at the ice had become a kind of madness and events leading up to the spring of that year did nothing to restore sanity. Rumours of war sent the value of seal fat skyrocketing, with the result that the Water Street crowd dispatched to the ice every vessel they could find, seaworthy or not, and crammed them to the hatches with men who had been told this was the *Eldorado* spring – *this* time they were bound to go home with their pockets stuffed with gold.

That spring, as for many years previously, the honorary commodore of the fleet was Captain Abraham Kean – legendary seal-killer who, before he gave it up in 1934, was to boast of having killed one million seals. He was a hard man, a driving man, and an obsessed man. His ship, the marvellous new *Stephano*, was the unquestioned queen of the fleet, and Kean was determined to fill her up – to bring in the greatest load of fat ever to enter St. John's harbour. With Captain Abe setting the pace it was a certainty that the other captains would risk heaven and earth in order not to be left too far behind in the race for the little silk flag which was the worthless but fiercely coveted prize given by the St. John's Chamber of Commerce to the high-lining sealing skipper of the year.

One of those who sailed to the front in the spring of 1914 was my father's shipmate, Skipper Llewelyn Kean. Skipper Lew was from Greenspond but was no relation to Captain Abraham Kean. Although he held his master's papers, he was unable to get a vessel of his own that year and so he shipped as a bridgemaster. That was a common thing, for in those years there were always more captains than there were sealing ships for them to command.

That was the first spring ever I sailed in one of the new steel ships. I had the luck to get a berth with Captain Billy Winsor in the Beothic; *a smart little vessel she was too. Billy Winsor was a smart man himself, a devil-may-care lad, all for the seals and a great hand for taking chances with his ship and his men if it would get him the fat.*

That year all the skippers, and the men too, were dead keen. Word had gone round that fat would fetch the highest price for forty years, and all hands looked to make a big bill if we found the patches.

The old wooden ships put to sea on March 10th, every last one of them as was still afloat – Bloodhound, Kite, Diana, Newfoundland, Terra Nova, Eagle, Thetis, Neptune, Ranger, *and* Southern Cross. *Some was bound to the front, but most, like the* Cross, *were going to try their luck in the Gulf. Because the steel ships were so much faster and abler in the ice, it was agreed they would give the wooden walls a start, so we didn't sail from St. John's until March 14th. All the steel steamers were bound for the front, for that is where the main patch lies. It was a grand sight they made, steaming out the Notch all in a line: the big* Stephano *in the lead; the* Florizel *and* Nascopie, *and then the smaller ships: the* Bell, Bon, Adventure, Beothic, Seal, *and* Sagona.

Most of them stuck close to old Abe Kean in the Stephano, *dogging the Old Man; but Billy Winsor was never a man to follow another skipper's course. When the fleet struck heavy ice off the Funks, and Captain Kean cut in for land to run inside toward St. Anthony, Billy cut north instead into the heavy stuff. My, how he drove that ship! Times I thought sure he'd tear the bows out of her, but in two days we was into the south corner of the main patch and not another ship in sight.*

It looked to be the finest kind of spring. By March 20th almost the whole fleet, wooden walls and all, were into the main patch along of we and killing seals for a pastime. The patch was long and narrow – I'd guess it to be fifty miles long and five or six wide. Right from the first we were high-liner, and Captain Abraham was in a fine fret because we were well up on him. By March 29th we had twenty thousand stowed below and another five thousand panned; but the Old Man had only eighteen thousand altogether. Still and all, every ship was doing very well except the Newfoundland. *Somehow or other, Captain Wes Kean, old Abe's youngest son, had gone astray and got his ship jammed into the worst sort of heavy ice about seven or eight miles from the whelping pans. Try what he would, he couldn't get clear, and his men were taking no seals at all.*

There were plenty of seals, but conditions weren't the best. One morning, the 23rd I think it was, we was working a patch when Skipper Billy, from the barrel, saw another big patch way off to the westward. He took back aboard two watches—a hundred men—including the one I was in, steamed out to the new patch and put us on ice while he went back to pick up the panned pelts and the rest of the crowd. Then the weather closed in, thick and wet, and when he started back he couldn't find us.

We didn't think to take much harm, because there were two or three other ships in the vicinity and we expected we could get aboard one of those if we was put to it. The *Florizel*, with Captain Joe Kean (another of the Old Man's sons), came handy to us to pick up some of his own men, and we started for her, but she veered off and went away full speed and was soon out of sight in the murk. Captain Joe saw us well enough but supposed our own ship would pick us up.

Dark come on with wind and wet snow, and it was not the best. The ice where we was, was going abroad and was soft anyway. The scattered fellow was falling in and when we'd haul him out he'd have to take off his boots and stockings and trousers, wring out the salt water, and pull them on again. He'd be so chilled the life was near out of him.

The drift got so heavy a man could hardly see his chum even before it come full darkness. We'd been on ice all day, every day, for about a week, and we were all beat-out. A good many of the men began to lose heart. There seemed to be no ships near us by then, though if there was, it would have been a job to find them anyway.

Sid and Willis White, belonged to Greenspond, came up to me and Willy said: "Lew, we got to get clear of this crowd. There'll be nary one of them alive tomorrow morning." I agreed we should branch off and try to find some tight ice and straighten away for the night. There was nine in my lot and we went off on our own. We found some good ice where there was still some live seals and a good many carcasses, and we set to work to build a circular shelter out of ice blocks and dead seals to keep away the wind.

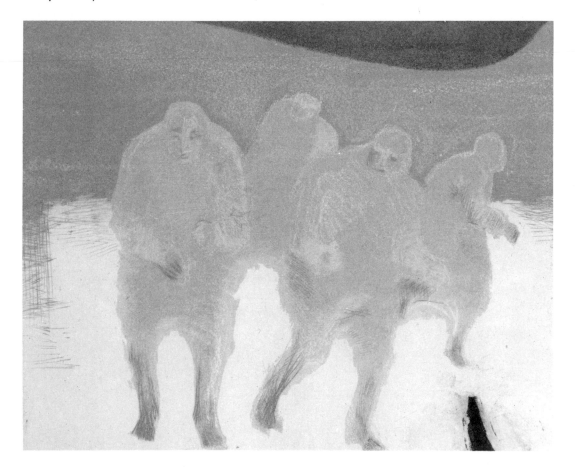

Now while we was at all this, Skipper Billy was still searching for us. He contacted the Florizel on the Marconi and asked had she seen any of his men. Skipper Joe come back and said he had, and Billy asked him to pick them up for the night. Joe agreed to try and, between the jigs and the reels, he did find the main crowd and took them aboard...and none too soon for some of them. But he never found us, and we never saw nor heard the ship.

Never mind that, we was all right. We had about thirty seal carcasses at our "door." We tore up our tarred tow ropes and frizzed them out for to light a fire. We fed it with shavings from our gaffs and poles until it was hot enough to melt seal fat and after that we kept it fair roaring with carcasses. They burned like a furnace and gave us all the hot roasted meat we had a mind to eat.

Every man went and got himself a live young seal and this is what we sat on all night. The seals didn't seem to mind. Every now and again they would open their eyes, look around, and go back to sleep. By morning they weren't white any more...they was just as black with soot and smoke as all the rest of us.

Morning came and the wind veered west, very strong and freezing cold. About midmorning, in the midst of a heavy squall, we heard a voice yell out: "HARD A STARBOARD!"–and there was the Beothic pretty near alongside our pan. Her lookouts had smelled the burning fat–'tis a terrible strong stink–and she'd steamed up on it until they saw our fire.

I tell you, we had a good time when we got aboard. Skipper Billy gave all hands a big drink of whiskey. I never minded being out that night– we was comfortable enough. But Sid White told me afterwards he never thought any of us would come through. It seems just before he come to me on the small ice, he and some other fellows were a bit apart when out of the drift there was the loom of something.

"Looked to I like a big kind of beast with long, sharp horns," Sid told me. "The snow gusted up in a minute, and it was gone when the squall cleared. A fearful bad sign, according to the old folk, for they says if you sees one of them ice spirits it foretells the death of a good many poor fellows."

Perhaps that's all a pack of nonsense, but all the same, what happened to us out there that time was well known right through the fleet, because of the Marconi; and I used to wonder afterwards whether the skippers took proper account of it. Certainly, Captain Wes Kean on the Newfoundland was the only man who never heard the news, for his was the only ship without a wireless.

I know one thing, though. Skipper Billy was right heedful where he put his men after that, and we were just as heedful to stay handy to our ship.

By Monday, March 29th, all the ships, with one exception, had been into the fat for ten days or more. Only the *Newfoundland* – the largest and most powerful of the wooden walls – was still out of it, still jammed fast in heavy, raftered ice, about eight miles southeast of the main patch where, in the light whelping ice, the rest of the ships were free to move about almost at will.

Captain Wes Kean's frustration and fury at having put his ship into such a situation had mounted to an explosive pitch by Monday night. At dawn on Tuesday the visibility was exceptional and when he climbed to the barrel he could see several ships on the northern icescape. Although unable to talk to them by wireless, he was sure they must be in the seals. He swung his glasses to the nearest one, the *Stephano*, commanded by his father, and saw that her after-derrick was hoisted vertically. This was a signal agreed upon between father and sons to show that the Old Man was working a good patch of seals. The sight was too much for the young skipper. Only twenty-nine years old, he had been made master of the *Newfoundland* four years earlier, largely because his father had pushed him up with Harveys. In order to refute the charge of favouritism, he had to bring in a good load of fat each spring. Now, the way things looked in this most important of all springs, he stood a good chance of having to come home almost clean. That was an intolerable prospect. Peering from the barrel into the beckoning northern wastes, he made up his mind. If the *Newfoundland* could not reach the seals, her men would have to go to the seals on their own feet.

Shortly before 7 A.M. all four watches, totalling 179 men, were ordered over the *Newfoundland's* side under the leadership of thirty-three-year-old George Tuff, the vessel's second-in-command.

" 'Tis a long haul and damned rough ice, Garge," Wes Kean told Tuff, "but the seals is there in t'ousands, sure. Go straight for the *Stephano* and report to Father. He'll put you onto the patches and tell you what to do. Doubtless he'll keep you aboard his ship tonight, and when the ice slacks off I'll steam over and pick up the men and the seals you've panned."

If Tuff had doubts about the wisdom of the plan he gave no sign; but doubts he must have had because, at the age of seventeen, he had been one of the survivors of the *Greenland* disaster. It had taken him months to recover physically from that experience and for years afterwards he had been plagued by frightful nightmares in which dead companions, frozen rigid, implored him to let them into his warm little house at Newtown.

The weather was extraordinarily fine that Tuesday morning – too fine, too warm, too calm by far, so thought some of the men who had heard from the bo's'n that the barometer was falling. " 'Twas a weather-breeder, certainly!" one of them remembered; and many were aware of a vague sense of unease as the long black column began snaking its way through the chaos of pressure ridges and raftered ice toward the tiny shape of the *Stephano*, hull-down to the north.

The going was even harder than Wes Kean had predicted. "I never saw worse ice in all my time," George Tuff remembered. After three hours of exhausting travel the attenuated column had only gone three miles from the *Newfoundland*. Those in the lead now came upon a scattered handful of whitecoats, and all the men halted gratefully while these were clubbed and sculped. When the long line moved on again it was incomplete. Some fifty men had detached themselves from it and, in startling defiance of the ingrained habits of obedience *and* amid shouts of "yellowbelly" and "coward" from their companions, had stubbornly turned about and headed back for their own ship.

When they reached the *Newfoundland* they were met by an infuriated Captain Kean who as good as accused them of mutiny and threatened them with the loss of their shares in the voyage. Subdued, strangely silent, they remained on the ice until his rage had run its course then, muttering something about "bad weather," they came quietly aboard and went below. Not one of them cared to tell Wes Kean the true reason for their return.

'Twas a bright, sunny morning when we left the Newfoundland. They was no reason to see nothing as wasn't there. But some of we saw something as had no right to be on the ice or anywhere at all on God's mortal earth! We come round a high pinnacle, and there it was...a giant of a man it looked to be, covered all over, face and all, in a black, hairy coat. It stood there, big as ary bear; blocking our way....Go forward in the face of that? No, me son! Not for all the gold as lies buried in the world!

115

It took nearly five hours of exhausting struggle before the remaining 126 men from the *Newfoundland* reached the high steel sides of the *Stephano*, which had stopped to let them come aboard. They had seen no more seals and a heavy haze had clouded the sky. A few glittering flakes of snow were already beginning to fall. The fine day was quickly coming to an end.

Before we got to the Stephano 'twas clear enough there was dirty weather on the go, and they warn't a man of we expected to go back on ice that day. We was certain sure the Stephano would be our boardinghouse. While most of the crowd went below for a mug of tea and a bit of hard bread, George Tuff went aft to see Captain Abraham Kean and get his orders.

The Stephano got under way again, and about twenty minutes later we was called back on deck. The snow was coming thicker, but the Old Man was up on the bridge waving his arms and bawling: "Newfoundland men, over the side!" Oh yiss, I can hear him yet. "Hurry up now, byes! Get out and get your seals!"

We hardly knew what to think about it, but the most of us supposed we was just going for a little rally, handy to the ship, and would be back aboard soon enough. But we was hardly clear of her when the Stephano swung hard around, showed us her stern, and drove off full steam ahead to the nor'ard. Young Jobbie Easton was along of me and there was a quare look on his face.

"That one's not coming back for we. She's gone for good!" Those as heard him began to crowd around George Tuff. "That's a lie now, ain't it, Garge?" some fellow asked.

"No, me sons," says George very low. "Captain Abraham's orders is for us to go and work a patch of swiles sou'west from here about a mile, pan the pelts, and then strike out for our own ship. He says as he's got men and seals of his own to look out for."

The snow was getting thicker by the minute, and any man who'd ever been on ice before knew what our chances was of finding the Newfoundland that night. Uncle Ezra Melendy pipes up and says: "Us'll never do it, Garge. 'Twill be the Greenland all over again." Then there was proper hell to pay. Some was calling on George to lead us back to the Stephano or chase after she. John Howlett stuck his chin out and told Tuff to stop wasting time and to start for the Newfoundland. "God damn it, Garge. This is no weather to be killing swiles!" Then John turned to us. "Byes," he says, "'tis time for we to give up this and go for our own ship!"

It come near to blows, but there was no changing George's mind. He had his orders from the Old Man and bedamned if he'd fly in the face of them. So off we went to find them seals and, afore we knowed it, the starm was on full blast.

On Tuesday morning, March 31st, one of the most savage storms of the year swept in over the southeastern approaches to Newfoundland and overwhelmed the island. Within a few hours the city of St. John's lay paralyzed beneath a tremendous snowfall, buffeted by hurricane winds. Ocean-going freighters laboured through towering seas offshore, seeking shelter, or lay hove-to, head to the gale, trying to ride it out.

During the afternoon the storm swept out over the northern ice and that vast plain became a faceless wilderness given over to whirling snow devils that obliterated everything from view. The storm caught nearly a hundred of Captain Abraham Kean's men far from their ship, for he had refused to believe the evidence of his senses, or of the plunging barometer, and had stubbornly continued to pile up seal pelts as if there was nothing else in life of any import. His men were lucky. The *Florizel* appeared, as if by magic, close to the *Stephano*'s men and, thankfully, they scrambled aboard. But the storm also caught one hundred and twenty-six of the *Newfoundland*'s men on ice . . . and there was no luck left for them.

Adrift in that raging chaos, on ice that began to heave and grind and shatter as the storm swell lifted under it, they were at least seven miles from their own jammed and helpless ship. What was more ominous, *nobody knew they were adrift*. Aboard the *Newfoundland*, Captain Wes Kean ate a good hot supper and went to his bunk, content in the belief that his men were safe aboard the *Stephano*. On the *Stephano*, the Old Man was preoccupied with wondering whether or not the storm would prevent him from overtaking that young upstart, Billy Winsor, and getting enough whitecoats to make him high-liner once again. If he gave any thought to the *Newfoundland*'s men, it was to assume they had reached their own ship. After all, that is where he had *ordered* them to go.

There was no way for anyone to discover the truth. Although all the other ships were fitted with wireless and could communicate with one another, the *Newfoundland*'s wireless had been removed before she sailed, by orders of her owners, A. J. Harvey and Company. As one of their directors was to testify later: "It did not pay to keep it aboard." Harveys did not feel that its presence added to the profits from the seal fishery. They were wrong. Its absence this spring was to deprive the company of considerable profit.

'Twas terrible...terrible, my son! After the starm came on I never saw a better chance for a disaster....We started back for the Newfoundland 'bout one o'clock, in a gale of wind, with the snow so thick and wet it was enough to choke a man. We struck east-sou'east looking for our outward track and found it, but 'twas too late by then. The ice was wheeling so bad the track was all broke up and there was swatches of open water everywhere. The snow was so heavy it lay thick on the water and 'twas a job to tell it from good ice. Before dark six or seven of the men had fell through and was lost....'Twas no use to go on....The men gathered round about on two or three of the biggest pans they could find, and they was

none too big at that, and built up shelters out of clumpers of ice. Then the snow changed to freezing rain, driving like shot till we was all drenched to the skin, but at least it warn't too frosty. I prayed 'twould keep raining, for if the wind backed to nor'ard and brought the frost, I knowed we'd no chance at all....

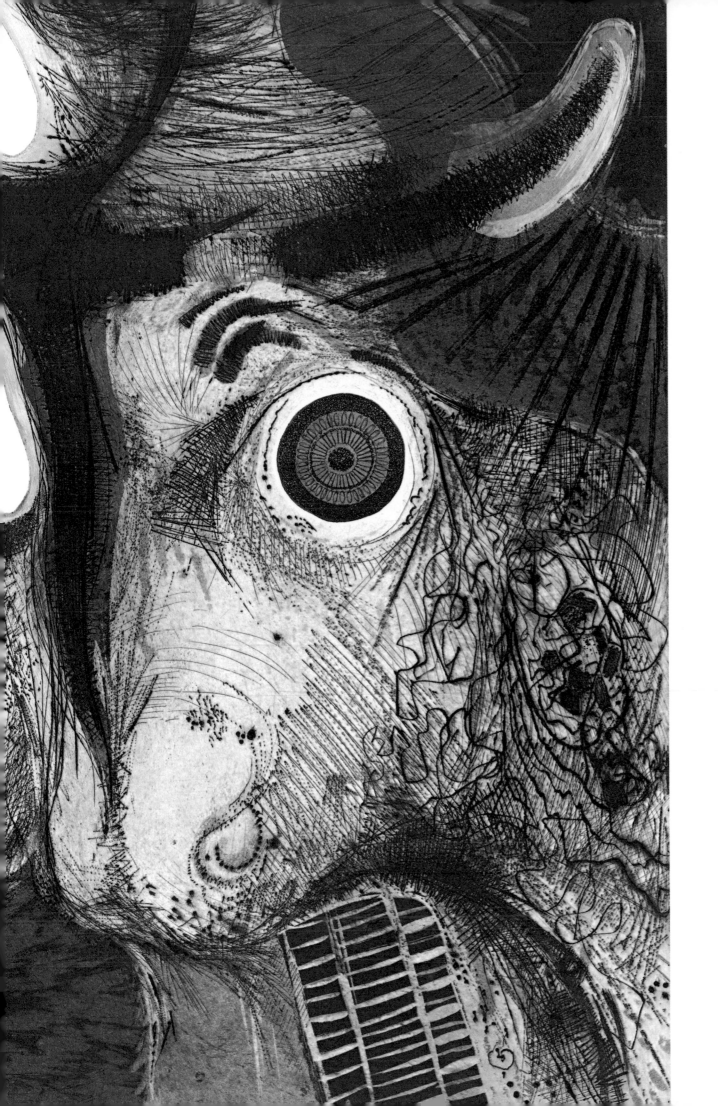

Lew Kean was safe aboard the *Beothic* that night and, as he said: "Thankful to God for it..."

I never saw worse weather at the front. I dare say there were few enough managed to sleep sound that night. The grinding and the roaring of the ice was enough to put the fear of the Lord into any man. Wild? I went on deck a time or two, and I don't know the words to tell what it was like. It was all a man could do to keep his feet, and the sleet cut into you like shot.

In the morning it was still blowing a living starm, and then it come on to snow again and the wind veered to nor'west and brought the white frost with it. That killed them altogether! The shelters those poor fellows had built was straight–like a wall–and no good at all when the wind come round. There was no seals where they was to, and they had nothing left to burn. Their clothes was pitiful poor, for it was a warm morning when they left their ship, and the most of them left their oilskins behind, counting to be aboard the Stephano for the night. For grub there was nothing but a bit of oatmeal or a pick of hard bread in the bottom of some fellows' nunny bags. A few had little bottles of Radway's Ready Relief–supposed to be a pain killer but, if the truth was out, only flavoured alcohol–good enough stuff, but there wasn't more than a glutch for every man.

Same as a good many sealers, they were mortal feared to lay down and take some rest. Believed they'd never wake again. That was pure foolishness...the worst kind! They spent the whole night on their feet, marching about like sojers, running around, pounding each other to keep awake...and they beat themselves right out. In the morning, when the frost took them, they were so done in they began to fall dead on their feet. Some even froze to death standing up.

About noon the snow let up and the sky cleared, but the wind was sharper and frostier than ever and the ground drift was like a cloud. If a man climbed to the top of a pinnacle he would be in clear air, with the sun shining on him, but on the ice he was near blind with the drift. In breaks in the storm, the few fellows as had the strength to climb the pinnacles could see some of the ships...the Florizel away to the nor'ard; the Stephano under way, and trying to pick up pans far off to the nor'east. Once the Bell come straight for them, close as three or four miles. Six men set out to walk to her, but they all perished, and the Bell, never seeing them, turned and steamed away. That took the heart out of the men as was left, like it was cut out with a sculping knife.

The devil of it was that not a one of we on any of the other ships knew they was lost. I tell you, when Harveys took that wireless out of the Newfoundland they killed those men better than bullets could have done.

Before dark come on, things was so desperate that George Tuff, with three of the master watches and a few other fellows, undertook somehow to get across that heaving mess of broken ice and reach their own ship. George had spied a glimpse of the Newfoundland from a pinnacle. She'd finally got clear of the jam and started steaming toward the Stephano, intending, I suppose, to pick up her men as Wes Kean thought was on his father's ship. When George saw her she was jammed again, but a lot closer to the men than before. Those fellows pretty near got to her, though how they stood up to it, the Lord knows. They was coming up toward her lee side...but all hands aboard her was looking out to windward where the Stephano lay. And then she burst out of the jam and hauled away for the Stephano, and those fellows just had to watch her go. That finished them entirely. They crawled into a hole in a pile of clumpers as night come down, freezing bitter cold and blowing a whole gale again.

Back on the two floes where the most of the men still was, it was even worse. The stories them poor fellows as lived through it had to tell was enough to freeze your blood.

...The weather was near zero and the snow blowing like a whirlwind ...you could look up sometimes through the drift and see the stars up there...down on the ice the men was dying...my first cousin, and my best chum, he lay down to die but I wouldn't let him do it. I punched him and hauled him about and jumped on his feet...that's how he lost his feet, I suppose. I got them all broken up, jumping on them. "Bye," I said to him. "Don't you die out here! Don't you give it to them at home to say you died out here on this ice!" But I had to go on kicking him...I nearly killed that poor fellow to make him live....

Some went crazy at the end of it, yelling and squalling and wandering off and never seen again. More died quiet, sitting or lying there, most likely dreaming of being home again...They saw strange things. One fellow come over to me and says: "Come in to the house now, me son. We'll have a scoff. The woman's just cooking up a pot of soup." I never saw him after. His eyes was froze shut with the ice caked on his face....

Uncle Ezra Melendy, as had lived through the Greenland disaster, was an old fellow but he wouldn't give it up. His legs was froze solid to the hips and he was crawling over the ice trying to keep close to we. He'd lost his mittens and his hands was froze hard like claws. He crawled up to me and says: "Me hands is some cold, byes." I went along his back trail a bit and found his mitts, but I couldn't pull them on his hands, all crooked up like they was. So I slit them with me knife and put them on that way. "That's good now," he says and crawls off. His body was never found afterwards....

Freddie Hunt never had his cap, and his boots was gone right off his feet. He had only a poor jacket of cotton made from a flour bag, but he was some determined not to die. Wednesday night he started to take the jacket off a dead man, but the corpse rolled over and says: "Don't ye do it, Freddie. I aren't dead yet!..."

The worst thing I seen was when I tried to get to another pan and I fell over a clumper. Only it warn't no clumper. 'Twas Reuben Crewe and his son, froze together, and the old fellow's arms tight around the lad, and the lad's head buried under his father's jacket...I recall the drift eased off about then and it seemed light as day and I looked around me and 'twas like being in a graveyard full of awful white statues...dead men all around....

Greenspond is a pretty place,
And so is Pinchards Island.
Me Ma will get a new silk dress
When Pa comes home from swilin'.

At the crack of dawn on Thursday morning Captain Wes Kean climbed to the barrel on the *Newfoundland*'s mainmast. The weather had moderated; the wind had dropped out and visibility was good. For some time he anxiously watched the *Stephano*, which was also jammed now but less than a mile distant to the east. He was looking for his absent men who should have been leaving the big steel ship to return to their own vessel. As yet there was no sign of life aboard the *Stephano* so he swung his glasses to the west to see if there were any seals in sight. He was electrified to see a small group of men staggering across the ice toward him in the pale half-light and, with sick comprehension, he knew what had happened. Kean very nearly fell from the shrouds in his haste to gain the deck, and when he reached it he was close to hysteria.

Half an hour later George Tuff and three others were being helped aboard their ship by a rescue party of horrified shipmates. These survivors of the lost party looked more like walking dead than living men. Tuff stood before his captain, weaving from side to side and barely able to mumble through cracked and bleeding lips.

"This is all the men you got left, Cap'n. The rest of them is gone. . . ."

At about the same time Tuff regained his ship, the barrelman of the *Bellaventure*, which was then steaming about looking for lost pans some miles to the northwest, saw what he took to be a small party of sealers belonging to some other ship. As he watched, he realized there was something wrong with them. "They looked right queer . . . like they was drunk, crawling and falling about." He called his skipper, Captain Robert Randell, and in a few minutes the *Bell* was crashing through the pack toward them under forced draft. Two of the figures were much closer than the others and at 9 P.M. the wireless began to crackle.

CAPTAIN SS BELLAVENTURE TO CAPTAIN SS STEPHANO.
TWO NEWFOUNDLAND MEN IN PRETTY BAD SHAPE GOT
ABOARD US THIS MORNING. REPORTED ON ICE SINCE
TUESDAY AND SEVERAL MEN PERISHED.

This report was picked up by almost every ship in the fleet and all those in the vicinity began to converge on the *Bell*. Soon hundreds of sealers were scattering across the pack laden with stretchers, food, and rum, searching for the lost party. By nightfall the *Bell*, magnificently handled by Captain Randell, had found and taken aboard thirty-five survivors, all frightfully frostbitten, including several who were thought to be beyond saving. The other ships had found nine more . . . *and that was all of the lost party ever to be found alive.*

At dusk the *Stephano, Bellaventure,* and *Florizel* came together alongside the stricken *Newfoundland.* The death ship's roll was read and the appalling scope of the disaster was finally revealed. Then the dead, the dying, and those who would survive, although crippled and disfigured for life, were all placed aboard the *Bellaventure* and she prepared to leave the ice for home. It appeared that she would be the first ship back to St. John's that year, but for her there would be no cheers from the crowded quay, no bellow of gunfire from Signal Hill. Below decks she carried the sculps of many thousands of prime seals – a fortune for her owners. On deck, twisted and contorted into ghastly postures, she carried the frozen bodies of seventy men who would go to the ice no more. Nine others of the lost party remained behind, already buried in the darkness of the icy sea.

So the *Bellaventure* departed . . . alone. Orders from the owners of the

remaining ships had been received by radio. They were to continue sealing. Many of the men on those other ships had lost cousins, brothers, even fathers in the disaster and now they came as close to violence as their natures would allow. When Captain Billy Winsor, whose ship was already log-loaded, tried to put his men on ice they flatly refused orders. "No, Cap'n," their spokesman told him. "Us aren't goin' swilin' in that graveyard. Not for the king hisself!"

One by one the captains gave up and took the cut for home . . . all save one. Captain Abraham Kean stayed out. He was implacably determined to better Billy Winsor's catch, and even when his own men mutinied he kept the *Stephano* in the ice.

"I seen him on the bridge when the *Bell* pulled away," one of his crew remembered. "Never had no eyes for her. He was spyin' to nor'ard on the lookout for swiles. More like a devil than a man, he looked up there. No doubt 'tis a lie, but they was some aboard was sayin' the Old Man'd think nothin' of runnin' the winches on one side takin' up sculps while he was runnin' 'em on t'other side takin' dead men off the ice."

133

She got up steam the twelfth of March and shortly did embark
To try her fortune in the Gulf in charge of Captain Clarke.
She carried a hundred and seventy men, a strong and vigorous race;
Some from St. John's and Brigus and more from Harbour Grace.
She reached the Gulf in early March, the whitecoats for to slew.
When seventeen thousand prime young harps, killed by her hardy crew,
All panned and safely stowed below, with colours waving gay,
The Southern Cross, she leaved the ice, bound up for home that day.

She passed near Channel homeward bound as news come out to say,
A sealing steamer from the Gulf, she now is on her way.
"No doubt it is the Southern Cross," the operator said,
"And looking to have a bumper crop, being well down by the head."

The last of March the storm came on with blinding snow and sleet.
The Portia, bound for western ports, the Southern Cross did meet.
When Captain Connors from the bridge, he saw the ship that day,
He thought that she would shelter off, up in St. Mary's Bay.
St. Mary's Bay she never reached, as news come out next morn.
She must have been all night at sea out in that dreadful storm.

No word has come from the Southern Cross, now twenty days and more,
To say she reached a harbour upon the southern shore.
The S.S. Kyle was soon dispatched to search the ocean round,
But no sight of the missing ship could anywhere be found.
She searched Cape Race and every place until she reached Cape Pine,
But of the ship or wreckage, the searchers found no sign.

The Southern Cross, out twenty days, she now is overdue.
We hope, please God, she'll soon arrive, all with her hearty crew.
We'll put our trust in Providence and trust to Him on high
To send the Southern Cross safe home and fill sad hearts with joy.

    —Sealers' song, 1914

In that ill-omened spring of 1914 most of the wooden walls went to the Gulf of St. Lawrence (to the *back* of the island) rather than to the front, partly to avoid competition with the steel ships and partly because ice conditions were always easier there since the heavy arctic pack was absent. Nevertheless, the Gulf voyage carried its own special risk. Between Cabot Strait and St. John's there lay some two hundred and fifty miles of open ocean — as wicked an expanse of water as exists anywhere, and at its worst in early spring when cyclonic gales thunder against the granite cliffs of Newfoundland's south coast. As old Captain Henry Dawes succinctly put it at the time: "You only needs to be a sealer to take a ship to the front, but to take one to the Gulf . . . Mister, you'd best be a sailor, and a damned good one at that!"

Captain George Clarke, in charge of the *Southern Cross*, was a jowler of a sealing skipper, but considerably less experienced as a sailor. He had no master's certificate and most of his previous experience had been limited to fishing schooners. Nevertheless, the *Southern Cross*'s owners gave him command of a 500-ton wooden steamer and a sealing crew of 174 men.

The *Southern Cross, Terra Nova, Viking*, and several others of the old ships had a lucky passage westward and took the Gulf ice on March 12th. They found the whitecoats almost at once and the great slaughter was soon under way. By Sunday, March 29th, Captain Clarke had proved his right to be called a jowler, for the *Cross* was log-loaded with about twenty-five thousand seals. Her holds were jammed full and several thousand pelts had been precariously penned on deck. That afternoon Clarke sent a radio message to Captain Bartlett, skipper of the *Terra Nova*, announcing that he was bound up for St. John's that same night and expecting to be the first ship home. Bartlett, whose vessel was also loaded, had "no mind to make a race of it." An experienced master mariner, he had taken thoughtful note of a drop in the barometer and he preferred to hold to the shelter of the ice until he saw what kind of weather was brewing.

The weather that was on its way was the same violent storm that killed so many of the men of the *Newfoundland* on the northern ice fields. Monday night, it caught the *Cross* in open water on the dangerous lee coast of southern Newfoundland. Another captain might have run for shelter, but Clarke chose not to do so despite the fact that his leaking, strained old vessel was grossly overloaded; was crank in a seaway at the best of times, and had almost no lifesaving gear aboard apart from a few flimsy wooden punts, which would not have lasted ten minutes in the great turmoil of wind and water that was already turning the ocean feather-white. The *Southern Cross* held to her course, corkscrewing into an increasingly savage sou'easter until she must have been acting more like a submarine than a surface ship. That was how she appeared to Captain Thomas Connors, skipper of the coastal freighter *Portia*, during a momentary and frightening encounter with the *Cross* a few miles off Cape Pine on Tuesday afternoon. The *Portia*, a new steel ship, was having all she could do to hold her own and was trying desperately to work up for shelter into St. Mary's Bay, when out of the driving scud a vessel suddenly hove into sight.

"A big, black, three-masted steamer came hell-bent out of the muck and damn near ran us down. She cleared our stern by no more than a dory's length. I only saw her for a minute, but there's no doubt she was the *Southern Cross*. She seemed half-seas under and so low in the water her decks was running green. Then she was gone."

It was the last time she was ever seen. Not a single trace of the *Southern Cross* or of her crew was ever found, except for a broken life belt bearing her name that washed ashore in Ireland many months later.

So ended the spring of 1914. The merchant princes of Water Street were the richer by the profits from 233,000 seal pelts. And the ordinary people of Newfoundland were the poorer by the deaths of two hundred and fifty-five of their best men.

One time every man, woman, and child as could walk would be on the docks and the cliffs to cheer the sealing ships back from the ice fields. This time 'twas all different. The people was there right enough, but they was quiet...some of them watching and waiting for a ship, and for men, as would never come home again. It seems to me as something broke in the heart of our old island that spring of 1914, and never rightly healed again in after times.

137

After the black spring of the *Newfoundland* the government was finally forced to pass laws giving some protection to the sealers. For the first time sealing ships had to pass classification examinations. When these were carried out in the spring of 1915 *only three* of the wooden walls scraped through!

The increased costs of keeping the old steamers in what was, at best, barely seaworthy condition cut painfully into the profits and most of the owners now began to lose interest in the hunt. The First World War had its effect too. All the new steel ships were chartered for war work, or sent abroad, and few of them survived to return to the Island when the war was over. In ever-dwindling numbers the remaining wooden steamers continued going to the ice, but they were dying fast. Between 1915 and 1931 the *Nimrod, Diana, Bloodhound* (third to bear that name), *Kite, Aurora, Erik, Viking, Stella Maris, Nord,* and the *Newfoundland* herself (hopefully renamed *Samuel Blandford*), all perished at the ice or on the Island's coasts and reefs.

A few new steel ships, including the *Imogene,* were built but they were cargo and passenger ships first and foremost and they went sealing only as a sideline. The truth was that the sealing game was fast playing out because the seals themselves were passing out of time. The harps and hoods had been unable to stand against the loss of forty or fifty million slaughtered during the preceding century. Still, during the thirties, there were a few lucky springs that almost made it seem as if the great days had returned – springs when the handful of remaining ships struck into a remnant of the main patch. It happened in 1933 when the *Imogene,* commanded by Captain Albert Blackwood, came wallowing in through the Notch, log-loaded with 55,600 seals and all flags flying to proclaim her victory. And for one more time the people of St. John's crowded up on Signal Hill, out on the Battery, and along the harbour quays to welcome the high-liner home. But it was only a last flicker of a sun already set.

At the end of World War II, what little was left of the sealing game passed into the hands of Norwegian interests. Manning new and deadly little motor vessels, they set out to clean up the last survivors of the harp and hood nations. A few Newfoundland coasters made occasional trips back to the ice, but theirs were hardly more than scavenging voyages to those northern floes that had, at long last, been almost scoured clean of life.

The great seal nations of the northern ice were gone, and the sealers of our Island followed, in the fading wakes of their own vanished ships. . . .

The wooden walls, and the men of the wooden walls, had accompanied the seal hunt to its zenith, and they descended with it. By 1933 only the *Ranger, Eagle, Neptune, Thetis* and *Terra Nova* remained afloat out of the nearly sixty wooden steamers which had taken part in the hunt out of Newfoundland ports during the preceding seventy years.

In 1942 they made their last voyage to the ice. The Second World War was then reaching full fury and no modern ships could be spared for the seal fishery but, once again, the price of fat had soared because of a war, and again there was money to be made out on the northern ice fields. Some of the St. John's merchants decided to take a chance – with other men's lives – and three grimy, splintered, decrepit old ships moved from their silent anchorage at the south side of St. John's harbour to the company quays. They were superficially fitted out, and one March morning slipped almost unnoticed through the Notch under the long grey guns of newly built coast forts. A friend, who was in the navy, saw them go.

I was in a frigate on the North Atlantic convoy run out of St. John's that spring, and we were inbound after a bitch of a crossing. It was foggy, as usual, and I was on the bridge when the Number One called out: "For Christ's sake, come and look at this!" I went out on the wing and there they were, like ghosts out of the past. The wooden walls! Three of them in line – belching black smoke, their lovely old spars still standing and still carrying their yards. There was the Terra Nova *and the* Eagle, *with the* Ranger *in the van. The* Ranger *dipped her flag to us and we saluted with our siren. I could hardly believe what I was seeing. They looked like they were a hundred years old. It was right out of another age; and I thought, "Bloody good luck to you, old timers. Bloody good luck ...you'll sure and hell need all you can get!"*

Old die-hard ships – and they were commanded by die-hard skippers of a vanished era, for no one else would have dared take those ancient relics to sea, to risk the submarines and, what was far more dangerous, to risk the northern ice once more.

In command of the *Ranger* was Captain Llewelyn Kean. Although born in 1889, Skipper Lew was still in his prime after thirty-five years at the sealing game. Here is his own story of that final voyage – the period that marked the end.

The Ranger. Yes...she was a grand old boat, you know. Took thousands and thousands of seals in her time. Built in Dundee in 1871 – white oak, greenheart, and Australian ironbark. She was only a little bit of a thing, not much bigger than a good-sized tugboat of today, with a 70-horsepower reciprocating engine, and fully rigged when she was young. Toward the end she still could carry sail, and there were times we needed it.

In 1938 I was second hand to Captain Sid Hill in the new Beothic, owned by Bowrings. They owned the Ranger too, and that spring she'd gone to the Gulf with Captain Moses Clarke and got into a devil of a jam, was nipped and pretty near sunk. Clarke got her back to St. John's somehow, clean she was, with nary a seal on board, and all broke up. He stepped ashore swearing he was finished with the seal fishery, and he meant it. Never did go back. Most people thought the Ranger was finished too, and not before time, but when Bowrings asked me if I'd take her out to the front and try and make some kind of a spring with her, why I said, "Fair enough, sorr." I doubt they cared if I got many seals. The thing was that if no one took her, she'd have had to be condemned.

It was well on in the season by then. The other ships had been at the ice for near two weeks. All I could get was about twenty-five men to go along of me, with old Skipper Ben Kean as second hand. We run into tight ice off the Funks, but I cut to the eastward and fooled around until I got a line on the other boats by listening in on the Marconi. After that it was all luck. We got into a corner of the main patch and took twelve thousand seals, and that was better than some of the other boats did that year. But we was in such heavy ice and had so little power we couldn't get clear again and was carried south for ten days until we was a hundred and twenty miles south of St. John's. Then the ice went slack and I straightened her out, nor'nor'east for the Notch. That night she began to leak like a salt basket. It looked like it was going to be a bad job, and I had a mind to go back into the ice so if we had to take to the boats we would have some chance. But the weather stayed civil, and the pumps wasn't losing ground too fast, so we held on and somehow brought her in.

There was the biggest kind of crowd waiting for us. I suppose nobody ever expected to see the old lady come back again. Women waved their aprons, and men and youngsters were all over the Battery yelling and shouting. When we got docked at Bowrings and they got emergency pumps onto her, I noticed that Skipper Ben looked poorly. I suppose it was a close thing. Anyway, him and me went into the cabin and I poured us both a big drink of rum. We downed it and I went ashore to report to the owners and that was the last time I saw Skipper Ben alive. His heart give out and he was dead within the hour.

Bowrings was well satisfied with what we done, and when I told them about Ben, they said: "I suppose you want to carry him home to Wesleyville?" I said: "Yes, sorr, we got to carry Skipper Ben home." So they told me to buy a coffin and charge it to the company. Real gentlemen, they was.

There was some as thought I was foolish to stay in that old tub, but anyway I took her out every spring after that. Mostly we had good voyages; and I learned her ways. One thing about her, she'd never leak while we was in the ice. But when she got into the blue drop, wouldn't she leak! The safest plan was to get into the ice quick as you could and stay as long as you could.

In the spring of 1942, on account of the war, only three ships went out. There was my cousin Charlie Kean in the Terra Nova, Sid Hill in the Eagle, and me in the Ranger. None of them vessels was fit to be at sea, I suppose – the Ranger was seventy-one years old that spring – so we agreed to stay in company. The crowd I had aboard was small, only fifty-five men, and the most of them old fellers or lads too young to jine the army; but they was yary – a good crowd.

It was a bad spring all round. Almost no ice at all and so, of course, no seals. We went down the Labrador as far as the Round Hills and found nothing; only we near got beat to pieces in a storm. So we ran back into Belle Isle Strait as far as Red Bay and anchored there a couple of days, pumping her out and trying to repair her a bit. Then we tried the French Shore. Nothing at all. So on we come to the south'ard, looking to find old seals moulting on what ice there was. There was a few around the Funks but the ice was too scattered to put men onto it, so we put out the boats and went swatching. Got a few hundred sculps the first day, but that night the glass began to fall like it had no bottom into it.

"Well, Albert," I says to my second hand. "We're going to have a starm, and that's all there is to it."

The three vessels was close together, but there was no harbour in sight and no heavy ice we could run into for shelter. If the wind come on from nor'east the way it looked, it was going to be hard times. We straightened out for Cape St. John to try and shelter up in Notre Dame Bay. The Eagle took the lead with the Terra Nova astern of us.

By midnight it was a howling nor'east gale and the old Ranger couldn't punch it. She began to give out. She opened up and leaked so bad the pumps couldn't come near it. Then, when we was about thirty miles nor'east of Cape Fogo, the headway came off her. She wouldn't answer her helm and swung right around and lay in the trough of the seas. I knowed what had happened, of course, before ever the chief engineer climbed up on the bridge to tell me the water was up to the boilers and the fires was out.

"Bad lookout, Cap'n," he says to me. "Nothing we can do now. The water is into the engine and the steam pumps is finished."

"Yiss, bye," says I. "That's right enough. We're in bad shape for certain."

We put all hands onto the hand pumps or hauling water out of her hold with barrels slung to the fore derrick, but that was only foolishness. She was rolling down to her gunwales with seas coming right across her, putting aboard ten times the water the men could get out. That would never do at all, so we bent on jib and foresail – it was all as her old standing

143

rigging would bear—and that gave us steerage way and we begun to head off before the gale. I says to myself: "Well, Lew, bye. Whatever she's going to do now, she's going to do." We just had to take it, whatever happened.

The men were played out entirely and most of them went below and fell into their bunks, too tired to care if they lived or not. Now the seas was coming right over her, end for end. They knocked down everything; beat up all our boats and swept the galley clean overboard, stove and all. The big greybeards coming in over her stern ran right through her. By dawn she was dead in the water and there was only five or six men still fit to help work the ship, and we needed four men on the wheel all the time. It was a bad enough job, and time for us to try and save ourselves.

I went to the Marconi shack and sent out an S.O.S., but the only one heard it was Skipper Charlie in the Terra Nova. He never knowed it then, but her time was almost up. In the summer of 1943 she went down in the Greenland Sea—the last of the old wooden steamers—the last of the fleet.

Anyway, I got him on the radio phone. He come back to say:

"Old man, nothing we can do for you. We got our hands full ourselves. Don't know what we're going to do ourselves. Too rough for any lifeboat to live now. You can't come to we and we can't go to you."

"Yiss, old son," I tells him. "I knows that right enough."

We could just get a glimpse of her now and again, half-mile abeam of us, and she was making terrible heavy weather of it, but not so bad as us, for she wasn't leaking and her engine was still working.

"Yiss. That's it then, bye," I told him. "We're finished anyway, Charlie. Too bad...too bad, but that's it now."

The wind got worse, close to a hurricane, a living gale, with snow and rain until there was nothing to be seen. The Terra Nova was gone, and we didn't know but what she'd sunk. There was no sight nor sound of Sid Hill and the Eagle. We was driving broadside for land now with all sails blown out, every scrap of canvas blown clean out of the bolt ropes. No steerage way at all, and the vessel full of water and lying like a log. If she'd been an iron ship she'd have gone under long before, but there was so much wood into her she somehow kept afloat all that day.

Toward evening she began to drive across the mess of sunkers and shoal water lying off Fogo Island. It was a hard sight, I'll tell you! Some of those sunkers was breaking and spouting fifty feet into the air. We couldn't do a thing for ourselves. All hands was crowded onto the bridge and into the bridgeway waiting for her to strike. As she was driving over one shoal patch, a sea broke clean over the whole ship and washed most of the Marconi shack overboard, putting us out of commission entirely; but the old Ranger never touched the bottom.

Finally we drove clear of the shoal ground, though our chances didn't look much brighter for that. It was coming on for night and we were driving down on a bold lee shore with no chance to make a harbour. We could see the cliffs of Change Islands to the south'ard and the water was flying up over the rocks as high as the heavens. No ship nor man could have lived a minute on a shore like that.

Just before dark we saw an edge of ice between us and the land. It was a field of ice the gale had packed into the channel between Change Islands and Baccalhoa Island. It was all broke up and slobby, but it was ice, and that was some better than black rock! And that's where we fetched up.

The Ranger rolled into the ice broadside. She rolled and she rolled, and all the time she hove in, and she hove in until she was a half-mile from the edge of the pack and into ice heavy enough to hold her steady. There was still a big surge under her but for all of that she was as sheltered as if she'd been alongside Bowrings wharf.

Well now, that put a different look on things. All hands turned to again and that crowd of old fellers and young lads worked until they got every drop of water out of her! They used pumps and buckets and barrels and whatever in hell they could find, and early in the morning of the next day they had her dry. And she stayed that way. Never leaked when she was in the ice–never had before and wasn't going to change her ways.

The next job was to get steam up. The engines had to be dried and cleaned. Whatever there was to burn, coal and wood, was soaked with salt water and the devil if it would burn. Then I remembered something the old skippers used to do. I told the chief to stoke her up with seal fat.

While all the men was working I was on deck looking at the mess. My, my, my, and wasn't she a hard-looking sight? But when I looked seaward I was some glad we was where we was to. The seas coming into the edge of the ice was running mountains high. Nothing could have lived out there. If it hadn't been for the ice, we'd have been all penned up and gone in the breach!

Sparkie managed to get his set going again good enough to send out a call, and who did he raise but Skipper Sid in the Eagle. Sid had drove up into Cobb's Arm a few miles to the west'ard of us and found a harbour, but he said he only just done it.

We held on all day, fixing her up, tightening her up, trying to do something with her; but toward evening the wind shifted southerly and the ice started to go abroad, sagging down on Baccalhoa. That was a poor business because the seas were still going right over that island, a hundred feet into the air.

I asked the chief if there was any chance to get a bit of steam and he went below and tried to turn her over but there still wasn't enough pressure in the boilers. The ice had all gone slack by then and we were beginning to drive toward open water, and it breaking white as milk. I told the chief to give her another try.

"If you can't do nothing with her now," I said, "get ready to leave her. Two hours from now there won't be a man left alive if we stays on board."

Well, he tried her again, and again it was no use.

"All right, byes," I told the crowd. "That's it now. Get out of her the quickest way you know!"

We had two smashed-up dories left and we put them over the side. The ice was all broke up, and heaving up and down, and surging in and out, and men couldn't live on it without they had something to hold onto. We put a line on each dory and a bunch of men would grab the gunwales and half-walk and half-swim through the slob till they got to safer ice, then we'd haul the dories back and send off another crowd.

It was time now for me to leave her, but I couldn't find the heart to do it. She'd been a good old thing, you know. Never killed a man, so far as I ever heard. Skipper John Dominie and Eli Kean wouldn't go without I went. I could see now she was bound to drive onto Baccalhoa and not God Almighty could save her, so at last I give the word.

By that time the dories was finished—swamped and useless—so each of us took a plank and over we went. When the sea hove in and the ice tightened we'd pick up our planks and copy like youngsters as far as we could get before it hove out and the ice went apart. Then we'd throw ourselves down on the planks till the ice hove in again. When we reached the safe ice there was a crowd of Sid's men had come overland to give us a hand. Our fellows went off with them to the Eagle for a warm bunk and some hot grub, but I hung on a while to watch her go.

She drove straight down on that island like a bird. When she was right under it a great big sea took her and hove her stern clear out of the water. Spars, funnel, and everything else went out of her like she was shaking herself clear of everything she had; and then she rolled down under and was gone. It was as quick as that, she went as quick as that....

Their names are legends still around the northern bays, but they are fast-fading legends. Even the giants among them, men like Captain Arthur Jackman, survive only in the tales told by a few old men who have overstayed their time. Jackman was more than a great sealer; he was a seer, and that is how Jacob Kelloway remembered him.

Built like a whale, he was, and a heart in him big as a bloody great puncheon. No smarter man ever jumped on a pan of ice.

"I don't care who was the best man here before I come," he used to say, "but I be the best man now!"

And he was too! A hell's-flame kind of a man. He'd curse you down one minute and give you a piece of his heart the next. And smart? One time his funnel blew to hell in a gale of wind and he built another out of wood and kept his ship steaming through the ice until he filled her to the hatches.

He didn't have no Sunday on his sealing calendar, but never mind, every night he called the whole crowd up for prayers on the main deck, fine weather, snow, or sleet.

Never wanted no rum on his ship. A bloody hard ticket, but a whole gentleman. A wonderful polite man too. One time he says to a man he was fighting: "Now please don't come handy to me or I'll just have to split ye with this hatchet!"

He was the head of them all, a great bear-looking stick of a man, honest as the sun and true as steel. "You men look to your work," he'd tell us, "and the Lord and me'll look to you!" Nothing born like him today.

A good many years after he swallowed the anchor and hauled ashore for good, I met him on Bowrings wharf one spring when the seal fleet was coming in from the ice. He said to me:

"Jacob, me son, take a good look at it now, for 'tis all going out afore long. This old island fed we people so long as we took no more'n we had to have. That's how it was when I was a youngster. Now 'tis all changed and gone abroad. 'Tis the gold they're after these times, and I don't say they'll give it up until there's nothing more to take. The seals will go under; aye, and the whales and the fish too. Then the people will have to get out of our old rock. The way she's pointing, they'll have to haul their boats, bar up their houses, and take to their heels. I believes 'twill be a bad lookout, me son."

2 William Lane Leaving Braggs Island
1971   16 x 20

7 Autobiography: Faces
1968   20 x 32

8/9 Wesleyville Remembered
1968   16 x 20

10 Summer on Braggs Island
1973   20 x 32

12/13 Fire at Sea
1970   20 x 32

14/15 Wreck off Braggs Island
1967   20 x 29¹/₂

16 Gram Glover Waiting
1972   20 x 32

18 Birth on Braggs Island (drawing)
1973   16 x 16

19 Two Dancers (drawing)
1972   14 x 16

20/21 Wedding on Braggs Island
1972   20 x 32

22 Aunt Mag Feltham on Braggs Island
1969   20 x 32

24 Funeral on Braggs Island (drawing)
1969   8 x 12

25 Island Funeral
1967   20 x 30

26 Aunt Rene on Stage (drawing)
1973   17 x 18

27 Four Mummers
1968   6 x 10

32 The Great Lost Party Adrift (detail)
1965   10 x 20

33 The Departure
1965   7 x 20

34 The Sign (detail)

35 Lost Party at Sea: The Sign
1965   20 x 22

36 Flying Kite (drawing)
1972   14 x 16

38 Sick Captain Returning
1973   20 x 32

39 Lost Party at Sea
1964   20 x 28

40 Schooner Sailing into Icefield (drawing)
1973   20 x 24

42/43 Monday Morning, March 1
1968   20 x 32

47 Captain Jesse Winsor
1973   8 x 10

48 Captain Llewelyn Kean
1971   7¹/₂ diam.

49 Captain Sid Hill
1971   16 x 20

51 Captain Solomon White
1971   20 x 32

52/53 Captain Edward Bishop with Officers
on the Bridge of the S.S. *Eagle*
1968   20 x 32

55 Captains Toasting the New Year (drawing)
1971   15 x 17

58/59 The Departure: Kean's Men Leaving
1969   20 x 32

60 Sick Captain Leaving
1972   20 x 32

62 Captain Abraham Kean (drawing)
1972   14 x 18

63 Survivor (drawing)
1968   18 x 24

64/65 S.S. *Imogene* Leaving for the Icefields
1973   20 x 32

67 S.S. *Imogene* with Crew on Ice
1967   20 x 30

70 Singing Sealer (drawing)
1972   12 x 14

72 Prayer Service Between Decks (drawing)
1971   15 x 17

75 Sealer's Dream
1968   16 x 20

77 Sealer's Dream–Outport
1972   8 x 10

79 Two Survivors Discovered (woodcut)
1964   12 x 17

We wish to thank G. P. Putnam's Sons
for permission to reprint
The Log of "Bob" Bartlett by
Capt. Robert A. Bartlett,
Blue Ribbon Books, New York,
copyright 1928.

The prints in this book are reproduced
through the courtesy of the Memorial
University of Newfoundland. They are
included in its Permanent Collection and
are from the Lost Party series, produced
from 1963 to 1973.

The drawings are from the collection
of the artist.

On the making of this book

Type was set by Cooper & Beatty Limited,
the book was prepared for lithography
by Herzig Somerville Limited,
printed by Sampson Matthews Limited
and bound by John Deyell Company